KEY

to

Wren & Martin's

High School
Grammar
and
Composition

By
EXPERIENCED TEACHERS

S. CHAND
AN ISO 9001: 2000 COMPANY

S. CHAND & COMPANY LTD.
RAM NAGAR, NEW DELHI-110 055

S. CHAND & COMPANY LTD.
(An ISO 9001 : 2000 Company)

Head Office : 7361, RAM NAGAR, NEW DELHI - 110 055
Phones : 23672080-81-82; Fax : 91-11-23677446
Shop at:schandgroup.com; E-mail:schand@vsnl.com

Branches :
- 1st Floor, Heritage, Near Gujarat Vidhyapeeth, Ashram Road, **Ahmedabad** -380 014. Ph. 27541965, 27542369.
- No. 6, Ahuja Chambers, 1st Cross, Kumara Krupa Road, **Bangalore** -560 001. Ph : 22268048, 22354008
- 152, Anna Salai, **Chennai** -600 002. Ph : 28460026
- S.C.O. 6, 7 & 8, Sector 9D, **Chandigarh** -160017, Ph-2749376, 2749377
- 1st Floor, Bhartia Tower, Badambadi, **Cuttack** -753 009, Ph-2332580; 2332581
- 1st Floor, 52-A, Rajpur Road, **Dehradun** -248 011. Ph : 2740889, 2740861
- Pan Bazar, **Guwahati** -781 001. Ph : 2522155
- Sultan Bazar, **Hyderabad** -500 195. Ph : 24651135, 24744815
- Mai Hiran Gate, **Jalandhar** - 144008 . Ph. 2401630
- 613-7, M.G. Road, Ernakulam, **Kochi** -682035. Ph : 2381740
- 285/J, Bipin Bihari Ganguli Street, **Kolkata** -700 012. Ph : 22367459, 22373914
- Mahabeer Market, 25 Gwynne Road, Aminabad, **Lucknow** -226 018. Ph : 2226801, 2284815
- Blackie House, 103/5, Walchand Hirachand Marg , Opp. G.P.O., **Mumbai** -400 001. Ph : 22690881, 22610885
- 3, Gandhi Sagar East, **Nagpur** -440 002. Ph : 2723901
- 104, Citicentre Ashok, Govind Mitra Road, **Patna** -800 004. Ph : 2671366, 2302100

Marketing Offices :
- 238-A M.P. Nagar, Zone 1, **Bhopal** - 462 011. Ph : 5274723
- A-14 Janta Store Shopping Complex, University Marg, Bapu Nagar, **Jaipur** - 302 015, Phone : 0141-2709153

S. CHAND'S *Seal of Trust*

In our endeavour to protect you against counterfeit/fake books we have put a Hologram Sticker on the cover of some of our fast moving titles. The hologram displays a unique 3D multi-level, multi-colour effect of our logo from different angles when tilted or properly illuminated under a single source of light.

Background artwork seems to be "under" or "behind" the logo, giving the illusion of depth. **A fake hologram does not give any illusion of depth.**

First Edition 1994
Reprints 1995, 96, 97, 98, 99, 2000, 2001 (Twice), 2002, 2003
Reprint with Corrections 2004

ISBN : 81-219-0400-5

PRINTED IN INDIA
By Rajendra Ravindra Printers (Pvt.) Ltd., 7361, Ram Nagar, New Delhi-110 055 and published by S. Chand & Company Ltd., 7361, Ram Nagar, New Delhi-110 055

BOOK I – GRAMMAR

EXERCISE 1

1. The cackling of geese— *Subject*
   saved Rome—*Predicate*
2. The boy—*Subject*
   stood on the burning deck—*Predicate*
3. Tubal Cain—*Subject*
   was a man of might —*Predicate*
4. Stone walls—*Subject*
   do not a prison make—*Predicate*
5. The singing of the birds—*Subject*
   delights us—*Predicate*
6. Miss Kitty—*Subject*
   was rude at the table one day—*Predicate*
7. He—*Subject*
   has a good memory—*Predicate*
8. Bad habits—*Subject*
   grow unconsciously—*Predicate*
9. The earth—*Subject*
   revolves round the sun—*Predicate*
10. Nature—*Subject*
    is the best physician—*Predicate*
11. Edison—*Subject*
    invented the phonograph—*Predicate*
12. The sea—*Subject*
    has many thousand sands — *Predicate*
13. We—*Subject*
    cannot pump the ocean dry—*Predicate*
14. Borrowed garments—*Subject*
    never fit well—*Predicate*
15. The early bird—*Subject*
    catches the worm—*Predicate*
16. All matter—*Subject*
    is indestructible—*Predicate*
17. Islamabad—*Subject*
    is the capital of Pakistan—*Predicate*
18. We—*Subject*
    should profit by experience—*Predicate*
19. All roads—*Subject*
    lead to Rome—*Predicate*
20. A guilty conscience—*Subject*
    needs no excuse—*Predicate*

1

21. The beautiful rainbow—*Subject*
    soon faded away—*Predicate*
22. No man—*Subject*
    can serve two masters—*Predicate*
23. A sick room—*Subject*
    should be well aired—*Predicate*
24. The dewdrops—*Subject*
    glitter in the sunshine—*Predicate*
25. I—*Subject*
    shot an arrow into the air—*Predicate*
26. The shepherd—*Subject*
    a barking sound .... hears—*Predicate*
27. a hermit — *Subject*
    On the top of the hill lives — *Predicate*

EXERCISE 2

1. Adjective—adds something to the meaning of the noun 'waters'.
2. Adverb—adds something to the meaning of the verb 'lives'.
3. Preposition—shows the relation between 'storm' and 'comes'.
4. Adjective—adds something to the meaning of the noun 'effects'.
5. Adjective—adds something to the meaning of the noun 'train'.
6. Adverb—adds something to the meaning of the verb 'weigh'.
7. Preposition—shows the relation between 'all' and 'battle'.
8. Preposition—shows the relation between 'yard' and 'me'.
9. Adverb—adds something to the meaning of the verb 'came'.
10. Verb—says something about 'Mohammedans'.
11. Noun—the name of something.
12. Preposition—shows the relation between 'is' and 'committee'.
13. Adverb—adds something to the meaning of the verb 'moves'.
14. Noun—the name of something.
15. Conjunction—joins the two parts 'I will watch' and 'you sleep'.
16. Verb—says something about 'they'.

EXERCISE 3

1. crowd—Collective
2. truth—Abstract
3. honesty—Abstract
4. class—Collective; pupils—Common
5. elephant—Common; strength—Abstract
6. Solomon—Proper; wisdom—Abstract
7. cleanliness—Abstract; godliness—Abstract
8. fleet—Collective; ships—Common; harbour—Common

9. class—Collective; grammar—Abstract
10. Nile—Proper; bank—Common; year—Common
11. committee—Collective
12. Nelson—Proper; victory—Abstract; Trafalgar—Proper
13. soldiers—Common; bravery—Abstract
14. health—Abstract; happiness—Abstract
15. bunch—Collective; grapes—Common
16. voice—Common
17. team—Collective
18. lie—Abstract
19. wisdom—Abstract; strength—Abstract
20. value—Abstract; time—Abstract
21. innocence—Abstract
22. room—Common; feet—Common; length—Abstract
23. days—Common; childhood—Abstract
24. streets—Common; cities—Common; crookedness—Abstract
25. verdict—Abstract; gentlemen—Common; jury—Collective

EXERCISE 4

A. (1) herd　　(2) army　　(3) crew
B. (1) laziness　　(2) cruelty　　(3) bravery　　(4) foolishness

EXERCISE 5

length	strength	width	breadth	height
youth	truth	wisdom	freedom	poorness / poverty
humility	shortness	goodness	pride	justice
decency	prudence	vacancy	bravery	vanity
cruelty	darkness	sweetness	novelty	sanity
bitterness	depth	humanity	quickness	ignorance
laughter	belief	choice	defence	freedom
obedience	service	movement	thought	sight
life	hatred	concealment	protection	judgement
expectation / expectancy	pleasure	seizure	advice	relief
excellence	action	flattery	punishment	pursuit
knowledge	starvation	departure	death	conversation
stealth	occupation / occupancy	perseverance	success	discovery
kinghood	infancy	motherhood	priesthood	friendship
manhood	ownership	agency	boyhood	captainship / captaincy

theft	roguery	heroism	bondage	rascality
Womanhood	regency	beggary	piracy	patriotism
bankruptcy	authorship	cowardice	pilgrimage	gluttony

EXERCISE 6

1. heavy—Adjective of Quality. (Descriptive Adjective)
2. several—Indefinite Numeral Adjective
3. Every—Distributive Numeral Adjective
4. live—Adjective of Quality
    better—Adjective of Quality
    dead—Adjective of Quality
5. Every—Distributive Numeral Adjective
6. same—Demonstrative Adjective
7. Several—Indefinite Numeral Adjective
    present—Descriptive Adjective
8. few—Indefinite Numeral Adjective
9. Neither—Distributive Numeral Adjective
10. What—Interrogative Adjective
11. Which—Interrogative Adjective
12. long —Adjective of Quality
    cold—Adjective of Quality
    infirm—Adjective of Quality
    old—Adjective of Quality
13. every—Distributive Numeral Adjective
14. several—Indefinite Numeral Adjective
15. much—Adjective of Quantity
    little—Adjective of Quantity
16. second—Definite Numeral Adjective
17. great—Descriptive Adjective
18. absent—Descriptive Adjective
19. glorious—Descriptive Adjective
20. small—Descriptive Adjective
    great—Descriptive Adjective
21. Good—Descriptive Adjective
22. little—Adjective of Quantity
    crooked—Adjective of Quality
23. hearty—Adjective of Quality
    royal—Adjective of Quality
24. furrowed—Adjective of Quality
    toilsome—Adjective of Quality
25. next—Descriptive Adjective
26. Some—Indefinite Numeral Adjective
27. cross—Descriptive Adjective
28. ill—Descriptive Adjective
    any—Adjective of Quality

EXERCISE 7

1. fearful	2. first	3. poor	4. serious
5. grand	6. violent	7. deliberate	8. sad
9. remaining	10. wide	11. medical	12. both
13. every	14. early	15. valid	16. constant
17. several	18. angry	19. five	20. eternal
21. ready	22. firm	23. plausible	24. silver
25. great	26. profound		

EXERCISE 8

easy book

pitiful ⎫
piteous ⎬ sight

timely help

heavenly vision

healthy climate

wealthy person

lovely garden

hilly region

needy people

greedy fellow

roomy building

costly watch

painful experience

doubtful case

wonderful weather

peaceful reign

childish argument

princely behaviour

mountainous country

ridiculous position

picturesque scenery

laborious task

wooden leg

pompous language

artistic device

progressive outlook

slavish mentality

contemptuous looks

tempestuous mood

sensible suggestion

quarrelsome neighbour

thoughtful speech

hopeful pupil

friendly terms

EXERCISE 9

Their marriage has been a *happy* one.

It was a *sad* day for Padma when her mother died.

Mohan is an *industrious* boy.

A *lazy* man accomplishes little.

Gopal got a *big* prize at the flower show.

This coat is *too* small for me.

A *soft* reply turns away wrath.

A *harsh* judge may become unpopular.

He is a *hard* man to please.

A *polite* man commands the love of all.

It was *rude* of him to behave like that.

Wise men must be respected.

You *were* foolish to reject the offer.

He is a very *rich* man.

My father is in *poor* health.

My sister is too *young* to go to school.

New brooms sweep clean.
Old men are usually wise.
I have known her for a *long* time.
He is too *short* to reach the picture.
He walked at a *quick* pace.
He is *slow* to make up his mind.
He is as *strong* as a horse.
His argument has many *weak* points.
He gave her *handsome* presents.
He is staying in *ugly* surroundings.
It was *clever* of the driver to avert a terrible accident.
Even *dull* pupils can understand this lesson.
It has been *kind* of you to help us.
One should not be *cruel* to animals.
Though he is seventy, he looks quite *healthy*.
He proved to be a *dutiful* son
We had a *distant* view of Mt. Everest.
I accepted the offer on *certain* conditions.

EXERCISE 10

a fierce storm; a sudden siege; sound sleep; a glorious victory; valuable advice; a violent blow; dead silence; slender hands; hot water; a reliable servant; a beautiful flower; a big city; a popular artist; an honest dealer; a harsh voice; a loving husband; a loyal subject; a pretty child; an ideal king; a faithful dog.

EXERCISE 11

good fortune; bad fortune; ill fortune; great fortune; small fortune.
a great man, a good man, a bad man, a famous man, a wicked man, a poor man, a rich man, a lucky man, an honest man.
good news; bad news; sad news; happy news; pleasant news; dreadful news; important news.
a violent storm, a fierce storm, a terrible storm, a fearful storm.
good health; bad health, ill health, poor health, indifferent health, delicate health.
a good novel, a great novel, an interesting novel, a humorous novel, a historical novel, a romantic novel, a detective novel.
good progress, rapid progress, slow progress, satisfactory progress, poor progress.
a large room, a big room, a small room, a spacious room, a dark room, a crowded room.
an unfortunate incident, an unhappy incident, an unexpected incident, a striking incident, an amusing incident.

■ EXERCISE 12 ■

courageous—cowardly, timid; many—few; wild—tame; hot—cold; lean—fat; heavy—light; costly—cheap; barren—fertile; beautiful—ugly; patient—impatient; honest—dishonest; civilized—uncivilized, savage; careful—careless; strong—weak; experienced—inexperienced; slow—fast; friendly—unfriendly, hostile; cruel—kind; soft—hard.

■ EXERCISE 13 ■

black, blacker, blackest; excellent, more excellent, most excellent; ill, worse, worst; gloomy, gloomier, gloomiest; mad; madder, maddest; safe, safer, safest; bad, worse, worst; unjust, more unjust, most unjust; gay, gayer, gayest; able, abler, ablest; dry, drier, driest; timid, more timid, most timid; ugly, uglier, ugliest; true, truer, truest; severe, more severe, most severe; exact, more exact, most exact; agreeable, more agreeable, most agreeable; difficult, more difficult, most difficult; little, less, least; few, fewer, fewest; numerous, more numerous, most numerous; merry, merrier, merriest.

■ EXERCISE 14 ■

(a)	1. latter	2. latter	3. later	4. latter	5. later
(b)	1. elder	2. older	3. elder	4. elder	5. older
(c)	1. eldest	2. oldest	3. eldest	4. oldest	5. oldest
(d)	1. farther	2. further	3. further	4. further	5. further
(e)	1. latest	2. last	3. last	4. latest	5. last
(f)	1. nearest	2. next	3. nearest	4. next	5. nearest

■ EXERCISE 15 ■

(Note :—Adjectives marked* have no degrees of comparison.)

1. poor—Positive; happier—Comparative; 2. such*; 3. less—Comparative; 4. slight—Positive; 5. live* stronger—Comparative; dead*; 6. same*; 7. wisest—Superlative; 8. best—Superlative; 9. simple-Positive; good—Positive; 10. slightest— Superlative; 11. sharper—Comparative; 12. small—Positive'; great—Positive; 13. less—Comparative; 14. some*; 15. no*; 16. open*; secret*; 17. such*; 18. other*; 19. Idlest—Superlative; 20. fair—Positive; 21. both*; 22. much—Positive; wholesome—Positive; 23. wiser—Comparative; 24. No*; good—Positive; 25. largest—Superlative; 26. heavier—Comparative; any*; other*; 27. good-Positive; 28. many—Positive; powerful—Positive; 29. longest—Superlative.

EXERCISE 16

Positive	Comparative	Superlative
shameful	more shameful	most shameful
clever	cleverer	cleverest
pretty	prettier	prettiest
interesting	more interesting	most interesting
hopeful	more hopeful	most hopeful
honest	more honest	most honest
important	more important	most important
patient	more patient	most patient
rude	ruder	rudest
delightful	more delightful	most delightful
stupid	more stupid	most stupid
attractive	more attractive	most attractive
heavy	heavier	heaviest
beautiful	more beautiful	most beautiful
fortunate	more fortunate	most fortunate
pleasant	pleasanter ⎤	pleasantest ⎤
	more pleasant ⎦	most pleasant ⎦

EXERCISE 17

1. better
2. hotter
3. prettier
4. idlest
5. sharper
6. dearer
7. richest
8. older
9. largest
10. best
11. worse
12. worse, worst
13. more ferocious
14. worse
15. tallest
16. driest
17. more useful
18. most useful
19. greatest
20. nutritious
21. proudest
22. best
23. least
24. lighter.

EXERCISE 18

1. better
2. longer
3. best
4. mightier
5. loftiest
6. larger
7. more beautiful
8. dearer
9. costlier
10. cleverest
11. older
12. younger
13. richest
14. greater
15. best
16. broader
17. cooler
18. highest
19. highest
20. more beautiful
21. best
22. greatest
23. mightier
24. most popular
25. most interesting
26. greater
27. thickest
28. lighter
29. easier
30. better
31. elder
32. utmost

EXERCISE 19

1. The pine-apple is less sweet than the mango.
2. Gold is less plentiful than silver.

3. This is the least useful of all my books.
4. Wolfram is one of the least common minerals.
5. All other fruits are less sour than the wild-apple.
6. Copper is less useful than iron.

EXERCISE 20

1. No other town in Malaysia is so old as Malacca.. (Positive)
    Malacca is older than any other town in Malaysia. (Comparative)
2. Meat is not more nutritious than soya beans. ⎤ (Comparative)
    Soya beans are not less nutritious than meat. ⎦
3. Jupiter is bigger than any other planet. (Comparative)
    Jupiter is the biggest planet. (Superlative)
4. Latif is more industrious than most other boys. (Comparative)
    Latif is one of the most industrious boys. (Superlative)
5. He would not as soon tell a lie as die. (Positive)
6. India is larger than any other democracy in the world. (Comparative)
    No other democracy in the world is so large as India. (Positive)
7. No other English poet is so great as Shakespeare. (Positive)
    Shakespeare is the greatest of English poets. (Superlative)
8. Very few Indian kings were so great as Samudra Gupta. (Positive)
    Samudra Gupta was greater than most other Indian kings. (Comparative)
9. No other animal is so ferocious as the tiger. (Positive)
    The tiger is more ferocious than any other animal. (Comparative)
10. No other island in the world is so large as Australia. (Positive)
    Australia is larger than any other island in the world. (Comparative)
11. No other metal is so heavy as lead. (Positive)
    Lead is the heaviest of all metals. (Superlative)
12. Some people do not have as much brains as money. (Positive)
13. A foolish friend is not so good as a wise enemy. (Positive)
14. The Marwaries are at least as enterprising as any other community
    in India. (Positive)
15. You do not know him better than I do. (Comparative)
16. I do not know him as well as you do. (Positive)
17. Bhim was stronger than any other man. (Comparative)
    Bhim was the strongest of all men. (Superlative)
18. Suresh is not more industrious than some other boys. (Comparative)
    Suresh is not the most industrious boy. (Superlative)
19. No other peak of the Himalayas is so high as Mount Everest.
    (Positive)
    Mount Everest is higher than any other peak of the Himalayas.
    (Comparative)
20. The cow is one of the most useful animals. (Superlative)
    The cow is more useful than most other animals. (Comparative)

21. No other country in the world is so rich as America. (Positive)
    America is richer than any other country in the world. (Comparative)
22. It is not so easy to practice as to reach. (Positive)
23. No other metal is so useful as iron. (Positive)
    Iron is the most useful of all metals. (Superlative)
24. Secret love is not so good as open rebuke. (Positive)
25. The Sears Tower is the tallest building in the world. (Superlative)
    No other building in the world is taller than the Sears Tower. (Comparative)
26. No other Indian was a greater orator than Sir Surendranath. (Comparative)
    Sir Surendranath was one of the greatest Indian orators (Superlative)
27. No other resort in India is healthier than Ooty. (Comparative)
    Ooty is one of the healthiest resorts in India. (Superlative)
28. The sword is not so mighty as the pen. (Positive)

EXERCISE 21

1. The little   2. A little   3. A little   4. The little   5. The little

EXERCISE 22

1. The few   2. The few.   3. a few   4. a few   5. The few
6. a few   7. The few   8. The few   9. a few .   10. A few
11. a few   12. a few   13. The few   14. The few

EXERCISE 23

1. a   2. an   3. An   4. The   5. the   6. a
7. the   8. a   9. a   10. a   11. an   12. The
13. The   14. a   15. a   16. a   17. the, a 18. he, the
19. a   20. an   21. The   22. The   23. an   24. a
25. an   26. an   27. a, an, a 28. a   29. a, the 30. the
31. an   32. the   33. the   34. a   35. the   36. an
37. an

EXERCISE 24

1. While there is life there is hope.
2. Her knowledge of medicine had been acquired under *an* aged Jewess.
3. *The* sun rises in *the* east.
4. The brave soldier lost *an* arm in *the* battle.
5. The doctor says it is *a* hopeless case.
6. I like to live in *the* open air.
7. Get *a* pound of sugar from *the* nearest grocer.
8. Set back *the* clock; it is *an* hour too fast.
9. The poor woman has not ten paise.

10. You must take care.
11. *The* Eskimos make houses of snow and ice.
12. Where did you buy *the* umbrella?
13. Have you ever seen *an* elephant?
14. Draw *the* map of India.
15. Do not look *a* gift horse in *the* mouth.
16. Have you told him about *the* accident?
17. Tagore was *a* great poet.
18. How blue *the* sky looks!
19. Who wishes to take *a* walk with me?
20. What *a* beautiful scene this is !
21. The musician was *an* old Mussalman.
22. The river was spanned by *an* iron bridge.
23. *The* moon did not rise till after ten.
24. Like true sportsmen they would give *the* enemy fair play.
25. They never fail who die in a great cause.
26. There is nothing like staying at home for comfort.
27. He likes to picture himself as *an* original thinker.
28. It is never *a* thankful office to offer advice.
29. *An* umbrella is of no avail against *the* thunderstorm.
30. I have not seen him since he was *a* child.
31. For Brutus is *an* honourable man.
32. Neil Armstrong was *the* first man to walk on *the* moon.
33. Man has no more right to say *an* uncivil thing than to act one.
34. We started late in *the* afternoon.
35. It is a strange thing how little, in general, people know about the sky.
36. *The* scheme failed for want of support.
37. *The* tiger, *an* animal equal to *the* lion in size, is *a* native of Asia.
38. Time makes *the* most enemies friends.
39. My favourite flower is *the* rose.
40. *The* time we live ought not to be computed by *the* number of years, but by *the* use that has been made of them.
41. Mumbai is *the* largest cotton textile centre in *the* country.
42. Men are too often led astray by prejudice.
43. *The* only best quality is sold by us.
44. What kind of bird is that?
45. Wild animals suffer when kept in captivity.
46. May we have *the* pleasure of your company?
47. It was *the* proudest moment of my life.
48. *The* Andamans are a group of islands in *the* Bay of Bengal.
49. He started school when he was six years old.
50. He neglects attending church, though *the* church is only a few yards from his house.
51. March is *the* third month of *the* year.

52.   Dr. Arnold was headmaster of Rugby.
53.   Man cannot live by bread alone.
54.   When will father be back?
55.   *The* Appenines are in Italy.

EXERCISE 25

1. she, her → Alice
2. they → doors
3. it → door
4. I, I → Alice
5. You, you → Alice
6. her → Alice
7. his → Hari; it → book
8. his → Karim; it—dog
9. his, he → Suresh
10. you → Rama
11. It → camel
12. she → lioness
13. its → horse
14. their → birds
15. he → thief
16. he → child
17. Thou → David

EXERCISE 26

1. Rama had taken his watch out of his pocket, and was looking at *it* uneasily, shaking *it* every now and then, and holding *it* to his ear.
2. The boys went into the garden, where *they* saw a snake.
3. Very soon the Rabbit noticed Alice as *she* went hunting about, and called out to *her* in an angry tone.

EXERCISE 27

1. they
2. I
3. they
4. me
5. me
6. I
7. I
8. me
9. they
10. I
11. me
12. I
13. him
14. I
15. him
16. him
17. him
18. they
19. them

EXERCISE 28

1. myself—Emphatic
2. himself—Reflexive
3. ourselves—Reflexive
4. myself—Emphatic
5. yourself—Reflexive
6. myself—Reflexive
7. themsleves—Reflexive
8. themselves—Emphatic
9. herself—Reflexive
10. themselves—Reflexive
11. himself—Reflexive
12. herself—Reflexive
13. themselves—Reflexive
14. yourself—Reflexive
15. myself—Emphatic
16. himself—Reflexive
17. ourselves—Reflexive
18. itself—Reflexive
19. themselves—Reflexive
20. ourselves—Reflexive
21. itself—Reflexive
22. himself—Reflexive
23. themselves—Reflexive
24. himself—Emphatic

25. himself—Reflexive
26. thyself—Reflexive
27. yourselves—Reflexive
28. himself—Reflexive
29. itself—Emphatic
30. myself—Reflexive
31. yourself—Reflexive
32. myself—Reflexive
33. myself—Reflexive

EXERCISE 29

Sentence No.	Relative Pronoun	Case	Antecedent
1.	that	Accusative	pen
2.	which	Accusative	answer
3.	whose	Possessive	woman
4.	which	Accusative	letters
5.	that	Accusative	house
6.	who	Nominative	man
7.	whose	Possessive	sailors
8.	which	Accusative	books
9.	that	Nominative	rat
10.	which	Nominative	books
11.	that	Accusative	book
12.	who	Nominative	children
13.	that	Accusative	knife
14.	that	Accusative	knife
15.	whom	Accusative	persons
16.	whom	Accusative	juggler
17.	that	Nominative	they

EXERCISE 30

1. who or that
2. that or which
3. who or that
4. what
5. which
6. which or that
7. who or that
8. what
9. who or that
10. that or which
11. what
12. that or which
13. who or that
14. whom or that
15. that or which
16. that or which
17. which or that
18. what
19. who or that
20. which or that
21. what
22. who
23. whom
24. what
25. what
26. as
27. as
28. who
29. what
30. as

EXERCISE 31

1. who or that
2. as
3. as
4. as
5. as
6. that or which
7. what
8. whom
9. which or that
10. what
11. whom or that
12. what...what

13. what	14. whom	15. what
16. that or who	17. that or which	18. who or that
19. as	20. whom	21. who or that
22. who or that....who or that		23. who or that
24. whom	25. what	26. that or which
27. that or which	28. whom	29. whom
30. whom	31. what	32. that or who
33. as		

[*Note* : In Exercises 32 & 33, alternative connectives are given in brackets.]

EXERCISE 32

1. I know a man *who* (*that*) has been to Iceland.
2. The thief *that* (*who*) stole the watch was punished.
3. Show the road *that* (*which*) leads to Delhi.
4. Here is the doctor *who* (*that*) cured me of malaria.
5. I met a boy *who* (*that*) was very cruel. (or : The boy whom I met was very cruel).
6. He *who* (*that*) does his best should be praised.
7. The man *who* (*that*) is honest is trusted.
8. My father, *whom* I loved, is dead.
9. The boy for *whom* the teacher sent came at once.
10. Wellington, *who* defeated Napoleon at the Battle of Waterloo, was a great general. (or : Wellington, who was a great general, defeated Napolean at the battle of Waterloo).
11. The dog bit the burglar *who* (*that*) had broken into the house.
12. Once upon a time there lived a giant *who* was very powerful and cruel.
13. We met a girl *who* (*that*) had lost her way.
14. Kalidas, *who* wrote some five dramas, is famous.
15. He is a rogue *whom* no one trusts.
16. The child *that* (*who*) came here yesterday is dead.
17. The child *whom* (*that*) I saw yesterday is dead.
18. I know the man *who* (*that*) stole the bicycle.
19. The man *who* (*that*) stole the bicycle has been arrested.
20. I have found the umbrella *which* (*that*) I had lost.
21. I saw a soldier *who* (*that*) had lost an arm.
22. This is the path by *which* he came.
23. The horse *that* (*which*) we saw was lame.
24. Those boys *who* (*that*) had been lazy were kept in.
25. I saw a girl *who* (*that*) was singing.
26. That boy *whom* (*that*) you see there bowls very well.
27. Here is the book *which* (*that*) you were asking for.
28. Here is the pencil *which* (*that*) you spoke to is deaf.
29. The man *whom* (*that*) you spoke to is deaf.
30. Coal, *which* is a very useful mineral, is found in Bengal.

EXERCISE 33

1. This is the building *which* (*that*) was built in a single month.
2. The letter *that* (*which*) you sent reached me this morning.
3. Karim, *who* is always idle, was punished.
4. I met my uncle, *who* had just arrived.
5. This is the house *that* (*which*) Jack built.
6. The boy *whom* (*that*) you see there is my cousin.
7. The ladies *whom* (*that*) I was speaking of have arrived.
8. The boys *who* (*that*) were watching the match clapped heartily.
9. The boy *who* (*that*) tells lies deserves to be punished.
10. I heard a song *that* (*which*) pleased me.
11. I heard some news *which* (*that*) astonished me. (or : The news that I heard astonished me)
12. I know a man *who* (*that*) has a wooden leg.
13. Here is a book *which* (*that*) contains pictures.
14. Give me the ruler *which* (*that*) is on the desk.
15. The bicycle *which* (*that*) Hari rode is a new one.
16. We got into a bus *which* (*that*) was full of people.
17. He has a friend *who* (*that*) is a clever artist.
18. He is a well-known man, *whose* generosity is the talk of the town.
19. The cat *that* (*which*) was pursuing the mouse caught the mouse.
20. Can I borrow the book *that* (*which*) you are reading?
21. The boy *who* (*that*) had won the first prize was very proud.
22. Little Red Riding Hood went to visit her grandmother *who* was ill in bed.
23. This is my cousin *whom* (*that*) I was speaking of.
24. He is cowardly boy, *whom* we all despise.
25. This is the cat *that* (*which*) killed the rat.
26. Those grapes *which* (*that*) you brought were very sweet.
27. Hari spoke to the soldier, *whose* arm was in a sling.
28. The captain praised Balu, *whose* bowling was good.
29. A man *who* heard me calling came running up.

EXERCISE 34

1. The boys gave a loud shout. The shout was heard across the river.
2. Bring me the book. It is on the table.
3. It was a wretched hut. She lived in it.
4. The boy fell off his bicycle. He has hurt his leg.
5. The elephant was sick. It died.
6. The farmer is cutting the corn. It has ripened.
7. Napolean died at St. Helena. The French honour him.
8. The crow dropped the cheese. The fox immediately snapped it up.
9. John is a diligent boy. He is my cousin.
10. I left a parcel here yesterday. Where is it?
11. I lost a book. I have found it.

12. The Japanese are a brave people. They were attacked by the Russians.
13. The boy made the top score in the last match. You see him there.
14. Dadabhai Naoroji was the first Indian to enter the British Parliament. He was a Parsee.
15. He is a poet. His works are widely known.
16. The Taj Mahal is the finest mausoleum in the world. It was built by Shah Jahan.
17. Last year we visited the Moti Masjid. It is a mosque of great architectural beauty.
18. The meeting was a great success. It was held in the Town Hall.
19. The rope snapped. It was old.
20. You have to do a task. It is easy.
21. Some people live in glass houses. They must not throw stones.

EXERCISE 35

1. Who 2. Whom/What 3. Who 4. Whom 5. Whom 6. What/ Who 7. Who 8. Whom/What 9. Whom/What 10. What/Whom 11. Whom 12. Which 13. Whom 14. Whom/What 15. Which 16. What/Whom 17. Which 18. Who/What 19. Who/What 20. Whom/What 21. Who 22. Who 23. Whom 24. Who/What 25. Whom 26. What 27. Which 28. What 29. Whom/What 30. What 31. Who 32. What/Which/Whom 33. What 34. Who 35. What 36. Which 37. What/Which/Whom 38. Whom 39. What 40. Which 41. Whom.

EXERCISE 36

Sentence No.	Verb	Transitive or Intransitive	Object, if the verb is Transitive
1.	shines	Intransitive	—
2.	cut	Transitive	his hand
3.	stopped	Intransitive	—
4.	blew	Transitive	his whistle
5.	rises	Intransitive	—
6.	stood	Intransitive	—
7.	ticks	Intransitive	—
8.	looked	Intransitive	—
9.	put	Transitive	your books
10.	rose	Intransitive	—
11.	sleeps	Intransitive	—
12.	crow	Intransitive	—
13.	lies	Intransitive	—
14.	burns	Intransitive	—
15.	changes	Transitive	all things
16.	eat	Intransitive	—
17.	Tell	Transitive	—

18.	sing	Intransitive	—
19.	hopped } sang }	Intransitive	—
20.	does (not) keep	Transitive	good time
21.	sat	Intransitive	—
22.	could (not) spare	Transitive	the time
23.	took	Transitive	shelter
24.	lifted	Transitive	the heavy weight
25.	wrote	Transitive	a letter
26.	lived	Intransitive	—
27.	know	Transitive	a funny little man
28.	fly	Intransitive	—
29.	fell	Intransitive	—
30.	shall bring	Transitive	my camera
31.	speak	Intransitive	—
32.	ran	Intransitive	—

EXERCISE 37

Sentences containing Transitive Verbs:
1. He sold his car.
2. Jack built a house.
3. I know his address.
4. Who broke the mirror?
5. Please close the window.

Sentences containing Intransitive Verbs:
1. He went home.
2. Birds fly.
3. The moon is shining
4. She arrived this morning.
5. He works hard.

EXERCISE 38

Sentence No.	Verb	Transitive or Intransitive	Object	Complement
1.	roars	Intransitive	—	—
2.	proved	Intransitive	—	false
3.	stood	Intransitive	—	—
4.	has fallen	Intransitive	—	sick
5.	continued	Transitive	braying	—
6.	is	Intransitive	—	cold
7.	are	Intransitive	—	out

8.	tried	Intransitive	—	—
9.	see	Intransitive	—	—
10.	fell	Intransitive	—	asleep
11.	is	Intransitive	—	hot
12.	are	Intransitive	—	Burmese
13.	seems	Intransitive	—	true
14.	hide	Intransitive	—	—
15.	hide	Transitive	their faults	—
16.	went	Intransitive	—	mad
17.	waited	Intransitive	—	—
18.	told	Transitive	a lie	—
19.	elected	Transitive	him	president
20.	found	Transitive	her	weeping
21.	struck	Transitive	the man	dead
22.	flew	Intransitive	—	—
	stole	Transitive	the cheese	—
23.	looks	Intransitive	—	threatening
24.	made	Transitive	him	general
25.	waited	Intransitive	—	—
26.	Sweep	Intransitive	—	clean

EXERCISE 39

1. Killed—Active.
2. Compelled—Active
3. was bitten—Passive
4. was caught—Passive
5. made—Active
6. was burned—Passive
7. made—Active
8. was bound—Passive
9. was killed—Passive
10. frightened—Active
11. is loved—Passive
12. was opened—Passive
13. see—Active
14. was obeyed—Passive
15. had been damaged— Passive
16. will be gained—Passive
17. chased—Active
18. was posted—Passive
19. is ploughed—Passive
20. was teased—Passive
21. drank—Active
22. struck—Active
23. takes—Active
24. was lost—Passive
25. has been posted—Passive

EXERCISE 40

1. The mouse was killed by the cat.
2. The tree was cut down by the man.
3. America was discovered by Columbus.
4. He was praised by his teacher.

5. The dog was teased by the boy.
6. The horse is fed by the syce everyday.
7. He was arrested.
8. A kite was being made by Rama.
9. The ball was caught by the boy.
10. A letter will be written by my father.
11. He will be conquered (by me).
12. I was kept waiting.
13. The lion was shot by the hunter.
14. The door was opened by Hari.
15. The thief was caught by a policeman.
16. The ball was thrown by Sohrab.
17. Twenty runs were scored by him.
18. I am vexed by your behaviour.
19. Character is revealed by manners.
20. A very remarkable discovery was made by him.
21. Great oaks are felled by little strokes.
22. The pony will be brought by Dhondu.
23. He is loved by everyone.
24. This picture has been drawn by my cousin.
25. Good news is expected.
26. The harvest is gathered by the farmer.
27. He was swindled by his own brother.
28. The inspector was pleased by the recitation.
29. The light has been put out.
30. Our army had been defeated.
31. Radios are sold here.
32. My bicycle has been sold.
33. It will soon be forgotten.
34. The theatre was opened only last month.
35. Smoking is prohibited.

EXERCISE 41

1. You and he were seen by us.
2. I was asked by name. (or : My name was asked by him.)
3. They were refused admission.
4. A doll was bought for the baby.
5. He was found guilty of murder.
6. Milk is often turned sour by a thunderstorm.
7. The ocean cannot be pumped dry.
8. The storm was seen approaching.
9. I am kept waiting.
10. The house was painted red.
11. I was told to leave the room.

12. I was promised a present. (or : A present was promised to me.)
13. The carriage will be ordered.
14. The cliff is being climbed by the boy.
15. Many things can be accomplished by a little effort.
16. You are being watched carefully.

EXERCISE 42

1. His father praised him.
2. George Stephenson built the first railway.
3. The noise frightened the horse.
4. Latif did not speak a word. (or : Latif spoke not a word.)
5. The boy's work pleased the teacher.
6. His friends took him to the hospital.
7. An earthquake destroyed the town.
8. People lined the road.
9. The people welcomed the President.
10. Kalidas wrote *Shakuntala*.
11. The fire damaged the building.
12. His singular appearance struck me.
13. Robots built those cars.
14. Spectators thronged the streets.
15. The wind blew down the trees.
16. Everyone will blame us.
17. A car knocked down the child.
18. This did not much surprise Alice.
19. It will greatly surprise him if they choose him.

EXERCISE 43

Active Voice :
Everyone *praised* the boy.
Columbus *discovered* America.
Someone has *stolen* my purse.
Passive Voice :
The boy *was praised* by everyone.
America *was discovered* by Columbus
My purse *has been stolen.*

EXERCISE 44

1. Babu was elected captain.
2. He was seen opening the box.
3. His words must be listened to.
4. Will those happy days ever be forgotten.
5. Who broke this jug?

6.   He was accused of various offences by his subordinates.
7.   Grapes cannot be gathered from thistles.
8.   Someone has cut off the telegraph wires.
9.   Alas ! his voice will be heard no more.
10. They held the 1998 Asian Games in Bangkok, Thailand.
11. Without effort we/one can gain nothing.
12. Let not the weak be insulted.
13. Wealth is desired by all and (is) acquired by some.
14. Why should you suspect me?
15. We keep the information on our computer.
16. We are told by the legend how its name was received by the castle.
17. I lost my watch.
18. Why were you defrauded of your earnings by him?
19. It will be learned/learnt by the public with astonishment that war is imminent.
20. His wife was made to do the work (by him).
21. He was appointed monitor.
22. His recovery was despaired of by the doctor.
23. They refused him admittance.
24. His warnings were laughed at and all his proposals (were) objected to.
25. He was regarded as an impostor and called a villain.

EXERCISE 45

1.   flows—Indicative, Simple Present
2.   shall answer—Indicative, Simple Future
3.   knew—Indicative, Simple Past
     was—Indicative, Simple Past
     had seen—Indicative, Past Perfect
4.   has been raining—Indicative, Present Perfect Continuous
5.   hear—Indicative, Simple Present
     has passed—Indicative, Present Perfect
6.   had finished—Indicative, Past Perfect
     came—Indicative, Simple Past
7.   takes—Indicative, Simple Present
8.   have been living—Indicative, Present Perfect Continuous
9.   Be—Imperative, Simple Present
10. shall have reached—Indicative, Future Perfcect
11. is—Indicative, Simple Present
     left—Subjunctive, Simple Past
12. told—Indicative, Simple Past
     had finished—Indicative, Past Perfect
13. forgive—Subjunctive, Simple Present
14. is waiting—Indicative, Present Continuous
15. pipe—Imperative, Simple Present.

16. am hoping—Indicative, Present Continuous
17. were—Subjunctive, Simple Past
18. do—Imperative, Simple Present
    dream—Imperative, Simple Present
19. shall have—Indicative, Simple Future
20. be—Subjunctive, Simple Present
    is—Indicative, Simple Present
21. had led—Indicative, Past Perfect
22. was—Indicative, Simple Past
    was—Indicative, Simple Past
23. have heard—Indicative, Present Perfect
24. had seen—Indicative, Present Perfect
    could (not) agree—Indicative, Simple Past
25. Beware—Imperative, Simple Present
    happen—Subjunctive, Simple Present
26. is cutting—Indicative, Present Continuous
    has ripened—Indicative, Present Perfect
27. wish—Indicative, Simple Present
    were—Subjunctive, Simple Past
28. would—Indicative, Simple Past
    stayed—Subjunctive, Simple Past

EXERCISE 46

1. move 2. saw 3. have sent 4. books 5. were playing 6. was driving 7. fell 8. saw 9. has 10. has been working 11. had done 12. hear 13. have known 14. have been studying 15. am doing 16. wants 17. shall be 18. watches 19. went 20. went 21. has been crying 22. saw 23. haven't seen 24. appears 25. was mending.

EXERCISE 47

1. wants 2. bought 3. have just cleaned 4. has been raining 5. have done 6. smell 7. is rising 8. has been 9. rarely comes 10. have been waiting 11. broke 12. have seen 13. have arrived 14. haven't seen 15. finished 16. was moving 17. had already started 18. had been walking 19. had seen 20. has changed 21. has packed 22. visited 23. haven't 24. had (Other items do not change.) 25. have never mananged.

EXERCISE 48

1. arrives 2. comes 3. will be sitting 4. am visiting 5. is going to rain 6. will have arrived 7. will visit 8. start 9. will be driving 10. begins 11. am going to sneeze 12. will have taken over 13. will pass 14. am going 15. will be seeing 16. am going to fall 17. is going to make 18. will be passing 19. is about to start 20. will have read.

EXERCISE 49

1. to fight —(Simple Infinitive) object of the preposition 'but'.
2. pray—(Simple Infinitive) objective complement
3. to eat—(Gerundial Infinitive) qualifies the adjective 'fit'.
4. sing—(Simple Infinitive) objective complement
5. to see—(Gerundial Infinitive) qualifies the verb 'am going'.
6. to advance—(Gerundial Infinitive) qualifies the noun 'order'.
7. work—(Simple Infinitive) used with 'must'.
    weep—(Simple Infinitive) used with 'must'.
8. to hear—(Gerundial Infinitive) qualifies the adjective 'sorry'.
9. to forgive—(Gerundial Infinitive) qualifies the adjective 'slow'.
10. to view—(Gerundial Infinitive) qualifies the adjective 'stern'.
11. to scoff—(Gerundial Infinitive) qualifies the verb 'came'.
12. to relieve—(Simple Infinitive) subject of the verb 'was'.
13. to blush—(Gerundial Infinitive) qualifies the verb 'is born'.
14. to soothe—(Gerundial Infinitive) qualifies the noun 'charms'.
15. to tell—(Simple Infinitive) objects of the verb 'seek'.
16. to retreat—(Simple Infinitive) subject of the verb 'was'.
    to advance—(Simple Infinitive) subject of the verb 'was'.
17. to enjoy—(Simple Infinitive) object of the verb 'wishes'.
18. to see—(Simple Infinitive) complement of the verb 'is'.
19. to be lost—(Gerundial Infinitive) qualifies the noun 'moment'.
20. to address—(Gerundial Infinitive) qualifies the verb 'rose'.
21. to dispute—(Gerundial Infinitive) qualifies the pronoun 'none'.
22. to laugh—(Gerundial Infinitive) qualifies the noun 'ability'.
23. to concentrate—(Gerundial Infinitive) qualifies the noun 'power'.
    [*Note* : The full sentence is 'I had better dwell......... ']
24. to see—(Gerundial Infinitive) qualifies the adjective 'quick'.
25. to speak—(Gerundial Infinitive) qualifies the adjective 'afraid'.
26. dwell, reign—(Simple Infinitive) used with 'had', which is understood.
27. hope—(Simple Infinitive) used with 'can'.
    to count—(Simple Infinitive) object of the verb 'can hope'.
28. To toil—(Simple Infinitive) subject of the verb 'is'.
29. to hear—(Simple Infinitive) put in apposition with 'it'.
30. to bribe—(Simple Infinitive) put in apposition with 'it'.

EXERCISE 50

1. He had not even a ten paise bit with him to buy a loaf of bread.
2. Every cricket team has a captain to direct the other players.
3. You must part with your purse to save your life.
4. His father went to Ajmer yesterday to visit the shrine of the saint Khwaja Pir.
5. The robber took out a knife to frighten the old Marwari.

6. I am not afraid to speak the truth.
7. The insolvent's property was sold by the Official Assignee to pay his creditors.
8. He works hard to earn his livelihood.
9. The strikers held a meeting to discuss the terms of the employees.
10. He has five children to provide for.
11. The old man has now little energy left to take his morning constitutional.
12. It was the Raja's custom (or : Rajah used) to allow no cows to be slaughtered in his terriroty.
13. He formed a resolution not to speculate any more.
14. England expects every man to do his duty.
15. She visits the poor to relieve them of their sufferings.
16. It is in his hobby to collect old stamps even at great expense.
17. The only way for him to escape punishment is to apologize for his misconduct.
18. To speak out frankly, I have no aptitude for business.
19. To impress his host he was on his best behaviour in his presence.
20. That young man must have been very foolish to squander away all his patrimony.
21.. It is highly creditable for him to have risen to eminence from poverty and obscurity.

EXERCISE 51

1. speaking—Present Participle, Impersonal Absolute.
2. Having gained—Perfect Participle, governing the noun'**truth**'.
3. approaching—Present Participle, attached to the noun'**storm**'.
4. Hearing—Present Participle, governing the noun '**noise**'.
5. considering—Present Participle, Impersonal Absolute.
6. beaten—Past Participle, qualifying the noun '**enemy**'.
7. Being dissatisfied—Present Participle, qualifying the pronoun '**he**'.
8. pouring—Present Participle, attached to the verb '**come**'.
9. Having elected—Perfect Participle, governing the pronoun '**him**'.
10. being—Present Participle, used absolutely with the noun '**traveller**'.

EXERCISE 52

1. laid—Past Participle; qualifying the noun '**fuel**'.
2. Being occupied—Present Participle, qualifying the pronoun '**he**'.
3. coming—Present Participle, qualifying the noun '**children**'.
4. benefit—Past Participle, qualifying the noun '**Michael**'.
5. read—Past Participle, qualifying the noun '**books**'.
6. learned—Past Participle, qualifying the noun '**lessons**'.
7. spoken—Past Participle, qualifying the noun '**word**'.
8. Seeing—Present Participle, governing the noun '**sunshine**' and qualifying the pronoun '**I**'.

9. Seizing—Present Participle, governing the pronoun **'him'** and qualifying the noun 'friend'.
10. Encouraged—Past Participle, qualifying the pronoun **'he'**.
11. Overcome—Past Participle, qualifying the pronoun **'he'**.

EXERCISE 53

1. The porter *opening/having opened* the gate, we entered.
2. *Starting/Having started* early, we arrived at noon.
3. We met a man *carrying* a load of wood.
4. The stable door *being* open, the horse was stolen.
5. *Seizing/Having seized* his stick, he rushed to the door.
6. *Taking/Having taken* up his gun, he went out to shoot the lion.
7. *Stealing/Having stolen* a piece of cheese, a crow flew to her nest to enjoy the tasty meal.
8. *Wishing* to pick a quarrel with the lamb, the world said, "How dare you make the water muddy?"
9. *Alighting/Having alighted* from the train, he fell over a bag on the platform.
10. *Meeting/Having met* his brother in the street, Nanak asked him where he was going.
11. *Being charmed* with the silk, my sister bought ten yards.
12. *Being delayed* by a storm, the steamer came into port a day late.
13. *Having resolved* on a certain course, he acted with vigour.
14. *Staggering* back, he sank to the ground.
15. The letter being badly written, I had great difficulty in making out its content.
16. *Having* no fodder, they could give the cow nothing to eat.
17. A hungry fox saw some bunches of grapes *hanging* from a vine.
18. *Hurrying* away with much haste, Cinderella dropped one of her little glass slippers.

EXERCISE 54

1. When he was going up the stairs, the boy fell down.
2. As I had lost my passport, I applied for a new one.
3. I once saw a man who was walking on a rope.
4. When he was walking on the roof, he slipped and fell.
5. As we had no guide with us, we lost our way.
6. As the stable door was open, the horse was stolen.
7. As he was paralytic, he could not walk.
8. I heard the noise and woke up.
9. Caesar was murdered and the dictatorship came to an end.
10. I worked all day and was fatigued.
11. We met an old Sadhu who was walking to Benares.

12. When his son had come of age, he entered into partnership with him.
13. He failed in the first attempt and made no further attempts.
14. I walked up to the front door and rang bell.
15. As winter came on, the grasshopper had no food.
16. As I was enchanted with the whole scene, I lingered on my voyage.
17. The enemy fought with the fury of despair and disputed their ground inch by inch.
18. The bandit mounted his horse and rode off.
19. The policeman ran with all his speed and was scarcely able to overtake the thief.
20. As I did not know my way, I asked a policeman.

EXERCISE 55

1. fighting—Participle, qualifying the pronoun 'he'.
2. reading—Gerund, object of the preposition 'by'.
3. Heading—Participle, qualifying the pronoun 'he'.
4. standing—Participle, qualifying the noun 'clown'.
5. Asking—Gerund, subject of the verb 'is'.
   answering—Gerund, subject of the verb 'is'.(understood)
6. Waving—Participle, qualifying the noun 'people'.
7. Walking—Gerund, subject of the verb 'is forbidden'.
8. Jumping—Participle, qualifying the noun 'thief'.
9. hoarding—Gerund, object of the preposition 'in'.
10. returning—Gerund, object of the preposition 'on'.
11. Amassing—Gerund, subject of the verb 'ruins'.
12. being —Gerund, object of the preposition 'at'.
13. playing—Gerund, object of the preposition 'in'.
14. spending—Gerund, object of the verb 'hated'.
15. Saroja trying to lie to her—Gerund, object of the preposition 'at'.
16. Praising—Gerund, subject of the verb 'is'.
    praising—Gerund, complement of the verb 'is'.
17. hearing—Gerund, object of the preposition 'of'.
18. managing—Gerund, object of the preposition 'by'.
19. winning—Gerund, complement of the verb 'is'.
20. visting—Gerund, object of the preposition 'in'.
21. singing—Gerund, subject of the verb 'was'.
22. playing—Gerund, object of the verb 'preferred'.
    studying —Gerund, object of the preposition 'to'.
23. teaching—Gerund , object of the preposition 'for'.
24. doing—Gerund, object of 'go on' (phrasal verb)

━━━━━━━━━━ **EXERCISE 56** ━━━━━━━━━━

1. wrote 2. blew 3. stood 4. flew 5. sang 6. sat 7. swam 8. shook 9. drove 10. bore 11. spent 12. felt 13. hung 14. flew 15. wore 16. struck, was 17. sowed 18. told 19. lied 20. came 21. ran 22. did 23. withheld 24. forgot 25. got 26. chose 27. threw 28. clung 29. went, hanged 30. knew 31. swore, was 32. tore 33. sank 34. hid 35. bade 36. lay 37. laid.

━━━━━━━━━━ **EXERCISE 57** ━━━━━━━━━━

It is years since I *saw him.* He has *seen* his best days.

Of late the custom has *fallen* into use.

The lot *fell* upon him.

The toast was *drunk* with great enthusiasm.

He *spoke* freely when he had drunk alcohol.

Marathi is *spoken* in the Maharashtra.

My patience *wore* out at last.

The inscription has *worn* away in several places.

In a fit of rage she *tore* up the letter

The country is *torn* by factions.

He has been *stung* by a scorpion.

The remark *stung* him.

You look as if you had *run* all the way home.

He *ran* for his life.

Once Sydney Smith, being asked his name by the servant, found to his dismay that he had *forgotten* his own name.

A better day for a drive could not have been *chosen.*

Computer technology has *come* a long way since 1970.

The old beggar was *bitten* by a mad dog.

A mad dog *bit* him.

The boy has *swum* across the Indus.

A cloud *swam* slowly across the moon.

I think he should have *written* and told us.

Honesty is *written* on his face.

He *laid* the book on the table. He had not *laid* a finger on him. They *laid* their heads together.

We *lay* beneath a spreading oak.

He has long *lain* under suspicion.

A beautiful shot from cover-point *took* off the balls.

He has *taken* a fancy to the boy.

Recently the price of sugar has *gone* up.

The argument *went* home.

The verdict *went* against him.

He had *begun* his speech before we arrived.

He *began* to talk nonsense.

Do as you are *bid/bidden*. He *bade* us good-bye.

He *bid* three hundred rupees for the pony.

Has the warming-bell *rung*?

I *rang* him up on the telephone.

Someone has *stolen* my purse. She *stole* his heart.

You must reap what you have *sown*.

Poor fellow! he was very hard.

They say he *drove* a hard bargain.

It seemed to me that she had never *sung* so well.

Our bugles *sang* truce.

He was much *shaken* by the news.

His voice *shook* as he spoke.

He is *eaten* up with pride.

In the end he *ate* his words.

Let us have *done* with it. I *did* my duty.

Home describes a race of men who *sprang* from the gods.

The ship *sprang* a leak.

Has Rustum *shown* you his camera.

He *showed* a clean pair of heels.

The explorers were *frozen* to death.

The blood *froze* in their veins.

I was *struck* by a stone.

It never *struck* me before that he was old.

I found upon inquiry that I had *mistaken* the house.

He *mistook* me for my brother.

Go, ask the ferrier whether he has *shod* the horses yet.

His path was *strewn* with flowers.

His voice gradually *sank* to a whisper.

And thousands had *sunk* to the ground overpowered.

Walking through the jungle, he *trod* on a snake.

He has *risen* from the ranks.

As his friends expected he *rose* tothe occasion.

On the arrival of a policeman, he *beat* a hasty retreat.

He *beat* the Afghans in a bloody battle.

It was not the only battle in which they were *beaten*.

The tempest *blew* the ship ashore.

Walking on the beach, we *caught* sight of a strange bird.

He has *caught* a Tartar.

After the storm we *had* a spell of fine weather.

I *met* a little cottage girl.

The poor fellow has *met* with many reverses.

We thought her dying when she *slept*.

He has *got* hold of the wrong end of the stick.
The faithful dog *led* his blind master.
And his disciples came to him, and *awoke* him.
I was soon *awakened* from this disagreeable reverie.
I was *borne* away by an impulse.
It has *stood* the test of time.
He has *sat* for the examination.
He says he has never *known* sickness.
I *knew* his antecedents.
The prisoner was *bound* hand and foot.
He has *broken* his collar-bone.
What is *bred* in the bone will not wear out of flesh.
I *strove* with none, for none was worth my strife.
He never *gave* me a chance to speak.
He is *given* to opium-smoking.
I *dreamed/dreamt* I was in love again.
I have *wept* a million tears.

EXERCISE 58

The story is tediously *spun* out.
I *meant* it for a joke. He was *meant* for a lawyer.
Suddenly the wind *arose*. There never has *arisen* a great man who has not yet been misunderstood.
Who *drew* the first prize? He has *drawn* a wrong inference.
The train *drew* up to the station.
I certainly *understood* you to make that promise.
I am afraid I did not make myself *understood*.
He was accidentally shot in the farm.
He is not known ever to have *shrunk* from an encounter.
There was no cruelty from which the robber chief *shrank.*
I noticed that he *smelt* of brandy.
The cart *stuck* in the mud.
The soldiers *swore* allegiance to the Constitution of India. He was yesterday *sworn* in as a member of the Legislative Council.
The waves *swept* the pier. The pier was *swept* away.
Plague wept *off* millions.
Often a lie has *cost* a life.
His folly *cost* him years of poverty.
A rupee *bought* twice as much fifteen years ago.
His enemies *crew/crowed* over his fall.
He *dealt* unfairly with his partner. The robber *dealt* him a blow on the head.
His rashness *lost* him his life. *Lost* time is never found again.
The man who yields to the fascination of the gaming-table is *lost.*
Sir, I have *found* you an argument; but I am not obliged to find you an understanding.

The picture *found* its way to the auction-room.

Christ *forgave* his crucifiers.

It is said of Akbar that he rarely *slept* more than three hours at a time.

His company is greatly *sought* after. It might be truly said of him that he never *sought* honour.

Adam and his wife *hid* themselves from the presence of the Lord God.

He *fell* never to rise again. A certain man went down from Jerusalem to Jericho, and *fell* among thieves.

He has *fallen* asleep.

He has *set* his heart on success.

The teacher *set* them an example.

He *died* at a ripe old age.

I *saw* her singing at her work.

He has *seen* the ups and downs of life.

The news spoiled my dinner.

He has *left* a large family. The police *left* no stone unturned to trace the culprits.

Three years she *grew* in sun and shower. Some of these wars have *grown* out of commercial considerations.

I have *thought* of a plan.

I *thought* of Chatterton, the marvellous boy.

He *became* the slave of low desires.

Not a drum was *heard*, not a funeral note.

He hopes his prayer will be *heard*.

He *fought* for the crown. He has *fought* a good fight.

His courage *forsook* him. He has *forsaken* his old friends.

The village master *taught* his little school.

They have *taught* their tongue to speak lies.

She *wrung* her hands in agony.

Any appeal for help *wrung* her heart.

He *wound* up by appealing to the audience to contribute to the fund.

He was *thrust* through with a javelin.

He has *said* the last word on the matter.

The bird has *flown* away.

The bird *flew* over the tree.

The murderer has *fled* to Australia.

The terrified people *fled* to the mountains.

During the night the river had *overflowed* its banks.

EXERCISE 59

1. shall 2. will 3. should 4. would 5. Shall 6. Would 7. ought 8. might 9. should 10. dare 11. didn't need to see 12. Could 13. was able to 14. used 15. mustn't 16. is to 17. needn't have waited 18. might 19. will 20. Would 21. would 22. was to have left 23. used 24. Shall 25. might

EXERCISE 59A

1. She may not be Anil's sister.
2. We may go to Shimla next month.
3. My sister could read the alphabet when she was 15 months old.
4. You must not wash the car.
5. You need not wash the car.
6. They must have left already.
7. May I use your phone?
8. I used to go to the beach every day when I was in Chennai.
9. He may pass his driving test easily.
10. He may/might have forgotten about the meeting.
11. Shall we visit Qutab Minar?
12. Nobody has answered the phone; they must have gone out.
13. He must be over seventy.
14. I needn't have met him (but I met him).
15. I didn't need to meet him.

EXERCISE 60

Sentence	Adverb	Modified Word	Its Part of Speech	Kind of Adverb
1.	ill	pleased	Adjective	manner
2.	again	Try	Verb	frequency
3.	too	shy	Adjective	degree or quantity
4.	very	early	Adverb	degree or quantity
	early	rose	Verb	time
5.	so	glad	Adjective	degree or quantity
6.	lengthwise	cut	Verb	manner
7.	Too	many	Adjective	degree or quantity
8.	quite	sure	Adjective	degree or quantity
9.	well	is said	Verb	manner
10.	once twice	have met	Verb	frequency
	alone	have met	Verb	manner
11.	far	off	Adverb	place
	off	is	Verb	place
12.	before	have heard	Verb	time
13.	somewhat	better	Adjective	degree or quantity
14.	much	am relieved	Verb	degree or quantity
15.	rather	long	Adjective	degree or quantity
16.	much	worse	Adjective	degree or quantity
17.	ago	arrived	Verb	time
18.	forward	urges	Verb	place
19.	all	in black	Adv. Phrase	manner

Sentence	Adverb	Modified Word	Its Part of Speech	Kind of Adverb
20.	kindly	were received	Verb	manner
	very	kindly	Adverb	degree or quantity
21.	out	is	Verb	place
22.	surely	expect	Verb	affirmation
	tomorrow	expect	Verb	time
23.	not	could speak	Verb	negation
	so	angry	Adjective	degree or quantity
24.	far	too	Adverb	degree or quantity
	too	hasty	Adjective	degree or quantity
25.	out	is	Verb	place
26.	enough	old	Adjective	degree or quantity
	better	to know	Verb	manner
27.	much	rather	Adverb	degree or quantity
	rather	not	Adverb	degree or quantiy
	not	would go	Verb	negation
28.	not	need roar	Verb	negative
29.	too	fast	Adjective	degree or quantity
30.	off	went	Verb	place
31.	no	worse	Adjective	negation
	before	was (under-stood)	Verb	time
32.	too	high	Adjective	degree or quantity
33.	somewhere	loose	Adjective	place
34.	differently	see	Verb	manner
	now	see	Verb	time
35.	not	was built	Verb	negation
36.	in	came	Verb	place
37.	not	(have) killed	Verb	negation
38.	not	do crowd	Verb	negation
	so	closely	Adverb	degree or quantity
	closely	together	Adverb	manner
	together	do crowd	Verb	manner
39.	no	better	Adjective	negation
	today	is	Verb	time
40.	needs	must do	Verb	affirmation
41.	not	do walk	Adverb	negation
	so	fast	Adverb	degree or quantity
	fast	do walk	Verb	manner
42.	not	put	Verb	negation
43.	round	order	Verb	place
44.	shamefully	has been treated	Verb	manner
45.	never	told	Verb	time

EXERCISE 61

This is the *very* book I want. (Adjective)
This book is *very* interesting. (Adverb)
The church is quite *near*. (Adjective)
The summer holidays are drawing *near*. (Adverb)
He is in all *ill* temper. (Adjective)
He speaks *ill* of his neighbours. (Adverb)
I was the *only* person wearing a coat. . (Adjective)
It took me *only* ten minutes to do it . (Adverb)
Keep the room *clean*. (Adjective)
I *clean* forgot about it. (Adverb)
He was ill for a *long* time. (Adjective)
How *long* have you lived here? (Adverb)
The train was forty-five minutes *late*. (Adjective)
He usually gets up *late*. (Adverb)
He is an *early* riser. (Adjective)
Come as *early* as possible. (Adverb)
My watch is ten minutes *fast*. (Adjective)
He speaks very *fast*. (Adverb)

EXERCISE 62

suddenly, more suddenly, most suddenly; often, oftener/more often, oftenest/most often; near, nearer, nearest/next; loud, louder, loudest; hard, harder, hardest; wisely, more wisely, most wisely; patiently, more patiently, most patiently.

EXERCISE 63

1. He *often* invited me to visit him.
2. I am determined *never* to yield this point.
3. I *already* know the answer.
4. We have *just* seen her *in the square*.
5. I *usually* have to reach the office *by 9.30*.
6. Will he *still* be *there*?
7. I shall meet you *in the park this evening*.
8. The train has *just* left.
9. "Can you park your car near the shops?" "Yes I *usually* can".
10. You *always* have to check your oil before-starting.
11. He is *never* in time for meals.
12. We should come *here one morning*.
13. He has *quite* recovered from his illness.
14. She *seldom* goes to the cinema.
15. That is not good *enough*.

16. You must *never* say such a thing again.
17. Suresh always arrives *at the office at 9 o'clock*.
18. He played the violin *brilliantly in the concert last night.*

EXERCISE 64

1. in—governs 'corner' 2. to—cupboard 3. for—crown 4. on—wall 5. through—town 6. by—five 7. to—Spain 8. under—tree 9. of—rocks; over—head   10. of—credit, renown   11. into—parlour; to—fly   12. into—street 13. with—dog 14. from—morn; till—night 15. after-wife; with-knife 16. by—brook; through—orchard 17. with—hair; under-oak; among—folk 18. with—lark; till—dark 19. By-gods 20. Under—chestnut tree 21. on-Sunday; to—church; among—boys 22. for— flowers; from—seas, steams 23. across—breast 24. beside—hill 25. around—porch 26. of—life; without—name 27. out of—fears

EXERCISE 65

1.	down—Adverb	2.	down—Preposition
3.	round—Preposition	4.	on—Preposition
5.	on—Adverb	6.	by—Adverb
7.	round—Adverb	8.	in—Adverb
9.	in—Preposition	10.	behind—Preposition
11.	behind—Adverb	12.	by—Preposition
13.	through—Preposition	14.	through—Adverb
15.	throughout—Adverb	16.	without—Preposition

EXERCISE 66

There is a garden *behind* the house. (Preposition)
The dog was running *behind*. (Adverb)
It is difficult to climb *up* the hill. (Preposition)
Lift your head *up*. (Adverb)
He arrived *by* air. (Preposition)
He hurried *by* without a word. (Adverb)
He walked *along* the road. (Preposition)
We were asked to move *along*. (Adverb)
There was nobody *in* the room. (Preposition)
Come *in*, please. (Adverb)
What do you know *about* him? (Preposition)
The children were rushing *about*. (Adverb)
I went *beyond* the museum. (Preposition)
What is *beyond*? (Adverb)
I have put the key *under* the bed. (Preposition)
He pulled up the covers and crowled *under*. (Adverb)
He was brought *before* the magistrate. (Preposition)
I have read that book *before*. (Adverb)
I can meet him *after* four o'clock. (Preposition)
Two months *after*, he resigned his job. (Adverb)

EXERCISE 67

1. along	2. under	3. in	4. of	5. of
6. on, to	7. for	8. by	9. over	10. by
11. to	12. without	13. to, in	14. under	15. since
16. for	17. by	18. of	19. of	20. from
21. with	22. to	23. at	24. for	25. from/off
26. for	27. into	28. since	29. at	30. from
31. by, with	32. into, to	33. by	34. under	35. over
36. among/by	37. against	38. from, to		

EXERCISE 68

1. for—concession 2. beyond—excess 3. before—time 4. After—time; of—separation 5. for—contrast 6. against—anticipation 7. through—cause 8. for—supposition 9. to—reference 10.. for—direction 11. by—direction 12. for—purpose 13. for—contrast 14. of—origin 15. with—concession

EXERCISE 69

1. at, in 2. at, in 3. with 4. by, in 5. at 6. in 7. since 8. by/before 9. at 10.. in 11. into 12. before 13. at, from 14. by 15. at, in 16. Since 17. Besides 18. since 19. in 20. with 21. by/beside 22. but/except 23. in, in 24. by, with 25. in 26. Besides 27. Besides

EXERCISE 70

We feel sympathy for persons *afflicted with leprosy.*
He was *sanguine* of success, but could not succeed .
These lines are so excellent that you should *commit* them to *memory.*
Quinine is a *specific for malaria.*
You should make *allowance for short weight.*
His dress was not *appropriate to the occasion.*
He decided to *abstain from animal food.*
I feel an *antipathy to dogs.*
Whenever he speaks, the audience are *convulsed with laughter.*
Contrary to expectation, I have got a first class.
Some animals are *infested with vermin.*
When he saw the wretched old woman, he was *touched with pity.*
His speech to the students is *subversive of discipline.*
Exercise is *beneficial to health.*
When I asked him to lend me his scooter, he said it needed oiling.
His reply was *tantamount to refusal.*
His service to the country is *worthy of praise.*
Columbus was *beset with difficulties* during his voyage.
We are *accountable to God* for our acts.
How can I *atone for* my *misdeeds.*

People *addicted to opium* cannot live long.

His appeal for mercy is *entitled to consideration.*

The crowd threw stones at the police, *heedless of the consequences.*

He was asked by his wife and parents not to join the army, but he was *deaf to their entreaties.*

Many people in this city have an *aptitude for business.*

He doesn't have much *incentive to hard work.*

He who is *sensitive to criticism* cannot get on well.

He acts as his conscience dictates, *indifferent to praise or blame.*

EXERCISE 71

He has great *affection* for his sister.

His *ambition for* power is likely to be realized.

We waited with *anxiety for* news of his safe arrival.

The boy made an *apology* to his teacher *for* his misbehaviour.

He shows an *aptitude for* research.

You shouldn't lay the *blame for* the accident upon me.

She offered herself as a *candidate for* the position.

He has great *capacity for* amusement.

Whenever he sees any sufferers, he is filled with *compassion for* them.

He received Rs. 10.,000 in *compensation for* the loss of his right hand.

I feel *contempt for* those who are cruel to their children.

He used to have a *craving for* opium.

I haven't much *desire for* wealth.

I have great *esteem for* my teachers.

His *fitness for* the post is questionable.

She has great *fondness for* music.

I agreed to be *guarantee for* his behaviour.

He has absolutely no *leisure for* sport.

She has a *liking for* detective stories.

He is no *match for* me in batting.

Hunger was the *motive for* the man's crime.

There is a great *need for* a book on poultry-rearing.

I have little *opportunity for* hearing good music.

He has a *partiality for* Chinese cuisine.

He is filled with *passion for* his secretary.

I feel *pity for the* refugees.

I have no *predilection for* cricket; in fact, I play tennis more than cricket.

We must find a *pretext for* refusing the invitation.

Hunger is the best *relish for* food.

He felt *remorse for* his misdeeds.

The French have a *reputation for* politeness.

 If I try to borrow Rs. 1,000 from the bank, will you stand *surety for* me?

EXERCISE 72

I have some *acquaintance with* Sanskrit.
The country entered into *alliance with* Russia.
I failed to strike a *bargain with* him.
That dictionary cannot stand *comparison with* this.
Your action is not in *conformity with* the law.
She is always at *enmity with* her neighbours.
Our country has commercial intercourse with Bangladesh.
His *intimacy with* that woman brought about his ruin.
The incident put an end to his friendly *relations with* the manager.

EXERCISE 73

She has an *abhorrence of* frogs.
I have full *assurance of* your success.
Mr. Ashok is in *charge of* the department.
He has a *distrust of* his subordinates.
I have no *doubt of* your integrity.
Only women with *experience of* office work need apply for the post.
Failure of crops has resulted in famine.
On October 2 there is *observance of* Gandhi's birthday.
They required *proof of* my nationality.
The *result of* a war is only destruction.
He died from *want of* medical aid.

EXERCISE 74

Only high officials have *access to* the Governor.
On his *accession to* the estate he gave a grand party.
Members of Parliament took an oath of *allegiance to* the country.
The *alternative to* surrender is death.
Starch is an *antidote to* iodine.
He feels an *antipathy to* this place.
His performance is an *approach to* perfection
The President gave his *assent to* the Bill.
The *attachment* of this clause to the bond is superfluous.
Pay *attention to* what I am saying.
As a *concession to* the public outcry, the Government reduced the tax on petrol.
These dirty alleys are a *disgrace to* the municipal corporation.
He takes a *dislike to* dogs.
Praise acts as an *encouragement to* the young.
There are generally *exceptions to* a grammar rule.
He hasn't much *incentive to* hard work.
The explorers' *indifference to* the dangers of the expedition is admirable.
I haven't received his *invitation to* the party.

Perseverance is the *key to* success.

His *leniency to* his subordinates landed him in great difficulties.

Venu's *likeness to* Madhav is so much that they are often taken for twins.

There is no *limit to* that child's imagination.

The agitation has become a *menace to* public peace.

Soldiers act in *obedience to* the orders of their superior officers.

I take *objection to* what you are saying.

The agitators caused *obstruction to* the traffic.

We were in *opposition to* each other on the question. ·

The *postscript to* the letter says that he will be on holiday from tomorrow.

In the *preface to* the book the author explains how the book should be used.

The lawyer made a *reference to* the woman's past conduct.

He has *repugnance to* playing cards.

The girls show great *resemblance to* each other.

This novel is a *sequel to* 'The Peasant'.

They at last made their *submission to* the enemy.

Who is first in *succession to* the throne?

There should be a *supplement to* this dictionary.

The sight of the watch on the table was a strong *temptation to* the house-maid.

He turned *traitor to* his friends.

EXERCISE 75

The doctor advised me *to abstain from* drink.

The General ordered *cessation from* firing.

I pray to God for *deliverance from* evil.

He traces his *descent from* an old Arabic family.

His speech was full of *digressions from* the main subject.

He had a miraculous *escape from* the aircraft crash.

She was allowed *exemption from* attendance at college.

This is the *inference from* his statement.

The sleeping pills gave him a short *respite from* the suffering.

EXERCISE 76

(a)   Bribery is *abhorrent to* him.

Your proposal is not *acceptable to* me.

His paintings are not *accessible to* the public.

I am *accustomed to* hard work.

He is *addicted to* many vices.

The remuneration was not *adequate to* the work done.

He lives in the hut *adjacent to* the park.

She is an *affectionate to* her step-son as to her own.

I'm *agreeable to* what you suggest.

The script of Kannada is *akin to* that of Telugu.

Corruption is quite *alien to* his nature.

He is fully *alive to* the dangers of the situation.

He is rarely *amenable to* advice.

This incident is *analogous to* what happened in Kanpur a week ago.

The rule is not *applicable to* this case.

His speech is not quite *appropriate to* the occasion.

Fresh air is *beneficial* to the health.

He is *callous to* the suffering of others.

This practice is *common to* Bengalis.

Nobody is *comparable to* him in thrift.

The criminal was *condemend to* life imprisonment.

(b)   Walking is *conducive to* good health.

   Is his action *conformable to* the law?

In his new place he found few persons *congenial to* him.

His life was *consecrated to* the relief of suffering.

What you have done is *contrary to* your father's wishes.

Your performance is very *creditable to* you.

He was *deaf to* the doctor's advice.

Your remarks about him are *derogatory to* his reputation.

Laziness is *detrimental to* success.

She is *devoted to* her children.

The recent cyclone has been *disastrous to* many crops.

The accident was *due to* careless driving.

Every citizen is *entitled to* the vote.

He was *equal to* the occasion.

Industry is *essential to* success.

Soldiers are *exposed to* risks.

A dog is *faithful to* its master.

His betrayal was *fatal to* our plans.

That idea is quite *foreign to* my principles.

The Committee is *hostile to* any more reform in education.

What you have said is *impertinent to* the occasion.

Reverses are *incidental to* a business.

(c)   I am greatly *indebted to* you for your help.

He is *indifferent to* praise or blame.

Training is *indispendable to* a doctor.

A father should not be *indulgent to* his children.

Disunion is *inimical to* national progress.

He is *insensible to* insult.

Mountaineers become *immune to* hardships.

What he said was *irrelevant to* the subject.

I am not *favourable to* the proposal.

Heavy rains at this time are *hurtful to* the crops.

Whether he comes or not is *immaterial to* me.

The judge is *impervious to* all entreaties.

These plants are *indigenous to* India.

If you don't obey traffic rules, you are *liable to* a heavy fine.

His speech was *limited to* only one aspect of the subject.

He is *lost to* all sense of shame.

We should be *loyal to* our country.

I don't think this point is *material to* your argument.

Lying is *natural to* him.

Sleep is *necessary to* health.

(d)   Pupils should be *obedient to* their teacher.

I am much *obliged to* you for your favour.

His behaviour was *offensive to* her.

He resides in the house *opposite to* mine.

This duty is *painful to* me.

Many professors are *partial to* women students.

This pronounciation is *peculiar to* Bengalis.

What you say is not *pertinent to* the subject under discussion.

They are *pledged to* secrecy.

Health is *preferable to* wealth.

The Committee's decision was *prejudicial to* many senior officers.

He was on sick leave *prior to* his retirement.

The deal will be *profitable to* all of us.

A man who is *prone to* idleness can accomplish little.

He was *reduced to* begging for money.

He is not *related to* me in any way.

What you say is not *relevant to* the subject.

The dirty old man was *repugnant to* me.

You are *responsible to* the Manager for the petty cash.

Lorry drivers are *restricted to* 40 miles an hour.

The Ganges is *sacred to* Hindus.

The plant is *sensitive to* light.

This man is very *serviceable to* me.

The boy is *subject to* colds.

That dress is not *suitable to* the occasion.

Mr. Ashok and his wife seem *suited to* each other.

The present list is *supplementary to* the list published before.

Mr. Raman's statement was *tantamount to* a confession.

You should be *true to* your promises.

EXERCISE 77

He was *absorbed in* his business so that he did not notice me.
One should be *abstemious in* food and drink.
She is *accomplished in* music.
He is always *accurate in* what he says.
He who is *assiduous in* his work is sure to succeed.
Your boy is *backward in* mathematics.
Aurangzeb was *bigoted in* religion.
His statement is *correct in* every particular.
The construction is *defective in* many respects.
Their diet was *deficient in* protein.
She is *experienced in* drawing.
You have not been *diligent in* your work.
The mountain was *enveloped in* clouds.
The boy is *fertile in* excuses.
He was *foiled in* his attempt to deceive us.
He has always been *honest in* his dealings with me.
He found himself *implicated in* a bribery scandal.
I am very *interested in* gardening.
He is deeply *involved in* debt.
You should not be *lax in* morals.
He is *proficient in* English.
You will be dismissed if you are *remiss in* your duties.
You ought to be more *temperate in* your language.
He is well *versed in* mathematics.

EXERCISE 78

I am not *acquainted with* that gentleman.
He is *afflicted with* asthma.
The expedition was *beset with* many difficulties.
He is very *busy with* his work.
Censorship is not *compatible with* freedom.
I am *compliant with* your wishes.
What you say now is not *consistent with* what you said yesterday.
Coleridge was *contemporary with* Wordsworth.
We should be *content with* what we have.
These imported blades, *contrasted with* the domestic product, are excellent.
I am *conversant with* all the facts of the case.
He was *convulsed with* anger when he learnt that his daughter secretly married.
He was *deluged with* questions.
Everybody was *disgusted with* his behaviour.
We were *drenched with* rain while returning home.
He is a man *endowed with* rare talents.

She was *fatigued with* the heavy work.

They were *fired with* zeal to fight for freedom.

She is *gifted with* a wonderfully sweet voice.

He was *infatuated with* a young woman whom he met in the theatre.

He was *infected with* influenza.

The kitchen is *infested with* cockroaches.

They were *inspired with* hopes of victory.

He is *intimate with* the secretary.

The President has been *invested with* full authority.

Overcome with fatigue, she collapsed.

The teacher is very *popular with* his students.

His words are *replete with* wisdom.

Last night he attended three parties and was *satiated with* food.

He is not *satisfied with* our work

I was *touched with* pity when I heard that he had died.

EXERCISE 79

He was *accused of* bribery.

He was *acquitted of* the crime.

She is *afraid of* dogs.

He is *apprehensive of* the risks.

They are not *apprised of* my arrival.

We were *assured of* his cooperation.

I am *aware of* my arrival.

He was *bereft of* reason.

He is always *cautious of* giving offence.

I am not *certain of* success.

This style is *characteristic of* Milton.

Water is *composed of* hydrogen and oxygen.

He feels *confident of* getting a first class.

He seems to be *conscious of* his guilt.

He was *convicted of* murder.

I am convinced of my error.

Mr. Joseph was *covetous of* his neighbour's land.

He was *defrauded of* most of his property.

She was *deprived of* any chance in life.

Our country is *desirous of* peace.

She was *destitute* of shame.

The story is completely *devoid of* interest.

I am *diffident of* my ability to do it.

We were *distrustful of* his motives.

He is *dull of* hearing.

The palace was not *easy of* access.

Why should you be *envious of* his success?
He walked quickly, *fearful of* weakening her.
He is *fond of* playing tennis.
One should not be *greedy of* power.
He was found *guilty of* forgery.
He quarrelled *with* his boss, *heedless of* the consequences.
I was *ignorant of* his departure.
Have you been *informed of* his intended marriage?
She is *innocent of* the charge of theft.
He rushed to save her from drowning, *irrespective of* the risk.
He is *lame of* his left leg.
He is never *lavish of* praise.
One should not be *negligent of* one's duties.
Such discussions are only *productive of* quarrels.
She is *proud of* her beauty.
He sent his son abroad for higher studies, *regardless of* expense.
The party is *sanguine of* success in the election.
He is *sensible of* the gravity of the situation.
I am *sick of* your excuses.
He is *slow of* understanding.
His speech to the employees is *subversive of* discipline.
I am *suspicious of* his intentions.
One should be *tolerant of* criticism.
She is *vain of* her beauty.
What you say is *void of* reason.
I am *weary of* his constant grumbling.
His modesty is *worthy of* praise.

EXERCISE 80

He is *anxious for* his sister's safety.
Kashmir is *celebrated for* its scenery.
The headmaster is *conspicuous for* his strictness.
It is *customary for* certain tribes to sacrifice animals to the gods.
This book is *designed for* high school students.
The ship was *destined for* London.
He is *eager for* promotion.
That man is not *eligible for* the post.
He is *eminent for* his patriotism.
You are not *fit for* the position.
My scooter is *good for* another five years.
I am *grateful for* your help.
He is *notorious for* his thefts.
God forgives those who are *penitent for* their sins.

I am not *prepared for* the examination.

It is not *proper for* you to behave like this.

Are you *qualified for* teaching French?

He isn't *ready for* school yet.

I am *sorry for* my inability to accept your invitation.

That amount will be *sufficient for* our needs.

The donkey is *useful for* carrying loads.

They are *zealous for* freedom.

EXERCISE 81

Mr. Mukerji has recently *acceded to* the Congress Party.

You have to *adapt* yourself *to* new conditions.

You must *adhere to* the truth.

You must do the work within the time I have *allotted to* you.

She *alluded to* her difficulties with her mother-in-law.

He *apologized to* the teacher for his misbehaviour.

I *ascribed* his rudeness *to* his fatigue.

He *aspires to* the position of Vice-Chancellor.

He readily *assented to* my proposal.

His art has *attained to* perfection.

Attend to what he says.

He *attributes* his failure *to* bad luck.

Does this umbrella *belong to* you?

Wealth does not *conduce to* happiness.

You must *conform to* the rules of the game.

Her parents did not *consent to* her marrying a Christian.

Have you *contributed to* the relief fund?

This road *leads to* the museum.

We *listened to* his speech carefully.

I *object to* your remarks about me.

It never *occurred to* me that he would become my boss.

I *prefer* death *to* dishonour.

I cannot *pretend to* an exact knowledge of the subject.

I don't understand whom you are *referring to*.

The conversation *reverted to* the original topic.

He *stooped to* bribery.

She had to *submit to* separation from her husband.

He *succumbed to* his injuries.

The bandits finally *surrendered to* the police.

The headmaster *testified to* the boy's ability.

The soldier *yielded to* the enemy.

EXERCISE 82

You should *abstain from* alcoholic drinks.
The old man fell down when *alighting from* the bus.
He *ceased from* smuggling watches.
The University *debarred* him *from* sitting for the examination.
He *derives* pleasure *from* teasing girls.
It is natural to *derogate from* an enemy's virtues.
In spite of repeated warnings, he didn't *desist from* smoking.
Kamala's hair style *detracts from* her apearance.
Under no circumstances does he *deviate from* the truth.
Hindi *differs from* English in many respects.
The speaker *digressed from* his topic several times.
Mr. Mukherji *dissented from* the opinion of the majority of the committee.
The judge managed to *elicit* the truth *from* the culprit.
I spoke to Mr. Ramesh when he *emerged from* his room.
The parrot has *escaped from* its cage.
Children under 10 were *excluded from* the performance.
You should *preserve* your papers *from* harm.
His father *prevented* him *from* seeing the film.
People are *prohibited from* smoking in the cinema.
An umbrella will *protect* you *from* the rain.
He *recoiled from* killing the snake.
He has not *recovered from* his illness yet.
Please *refrain from* smoking in this room.

EXERCISE 83

Tom does not *associate with* naughty boys.
You should *bear with* the child while he is ill.
My interests *clash with* my brother's.
His tastes *coincide with* his wife's.
You should *comply with* the rules.
We *condole with* you on your bereavement.
He is used to *coping with* difficulties.
His actions rarely *correspond with* his words.
I was wrong to *credit* him *with* sense.
On being re-elected the President was *deluged with* congratulatory telegrams.
The lunch *disagreed with* me : I feel sick.
I am well enough to *dispense with* the doctor's services.
I *expostulated with* Gopi about his decision.
Fill the glass *with* lemonade.
Grapple with the problem ; you should be able to solve it.
Cassius *intrigued with* Brutus against Casear.
Don't *meddle with* the radio.
I don't like to *part with* my scooter.

She is always *quarrelling with* her husband.

I *remonstrated with* him about his foolish behaviour.

He is wise enough to *side with* the stronger party.

I *sympathise with* you in your difficulties.

Don't *trifle with* the girl's affections.

Gopal *vied with* Madhav for the first prize.

EXERCISE 84

The jury *acquitted* him *of* the crime.

Beware of pickpockets.

He *boasts of* being the best wrestler in the town.

He *complained of* having heavy work.

I *despaired of* finding my lost watch.

She *died of* cholera.

My mother *disapproves of* my getting up late.

I must *dispose of* the rubbish.

The thief *divested* the child *of* all her jewels.

I had always *dreamed of* a trip to this country.

The doctor assured her that he would *heal* her *of* the disease in a few days.

Don't *judge of* a man by his appearance.

He *repents of* having disobeyed his father.

Brave men *taste of* death but once.

EXERCISE 85

He *atoned for* the sin by giving alms to the poor.

He is *canvassing for* the Congress candidate.

I don't much *care for* mangoes.

The pupils are *clamouring for* a holiday.

I *feel for* that poor widow.

Let us *hope for* the best.

They *mourned for* their dead leader.

The exiles were *pining for* home.

Soon after hearing the news of his mother's illness, he *started for* his home town.

He *stipulated for* immediate supply of the articles.

He *sued* the company *for* damages to his property.

How he *wished for* a glass of wine!

The child *yearns for* the sight of its mother.

EXERCISE 86

He *acquiesced in* my proposal.

Children like *dabbling in* water.

He *delights in* teasing children.

He is *employed in* a factory.
A number of men were *enlisted in* the army.
He *excels* me in hockey.
He *failed in* the examination.
He *gloried in* his victory.
The country is *increasing in* population.
Don't *indulge in* too much candy.
You should not *involve* yourself *in* the matter.
If you *preserve* in your studies, you will get a first class.
The boy *persists* in biting his nails.

EXERCISE 87

The teacher *commented on* Gopi's progress.
She finally *decided on* the blue sari.
The committee is *deliberating on* the matter.
He still *depends on* his parents for support.
He is *determined on* joining the army.
Whenever I meet him he *dwells on* his misfortunes.
My uncle has *embarked on* a new enterprise.
I don't like to *encroach on* your time.
We want you to *enlarge on* this matter.
A government *imposes* certain restrictions *on* its citizens.
I *insist on* your attending the party.
Let's not *intrude on* his privacy.
He *resolved on* proving his friend's innocence.
Many yogis *subsist on* leaves and fruits.
The children *trampled on* the flower beds.

EXERCISE 88

1. to 2. with, in 3. with, over 4. with 5. with 6. to 7. of 8. with 9. with
10. to 11. from 12. of 13. of 14. to 15. of 16. to 17. in 18. to 19. to
20. with, in 21. to 22. to, for 23. of 24. of 25. on 26. of 27. from 28. on
29. with, for 30. to 31. with 32. to 33. by 34. at 35. to 36. of 37. of 38. with
39. in 40. on 41. in 42. to, for 43. in 44. of 45. in 46. with 47. to 48. in
49. of 50. of 51. of 52. for 53. in 54. to 55. to 56. of 57. from 58. to 59. of
60. with.

EXERCISE 89

1. to 2. from 3. to 4. to 5. on 6. of 7. with 8. in 9. with 10. for 11. for
12. to 13. to 14. to 15. to 16. to 17. to 18. for 19. of 20. from 21. to
22. to 23. of 24. to 25. in 26. to 27. to 28. to 29. with 30. at 31. to 32. to
33. of 34. to 35. of 36. to 37. to 38. with, at 39. with 40. to 41. with 42. for
43. of 44. under 45. at 46. to 47. in 48. to 49. on 50. with 51. to 52. on 53. on
54. at 55. with 56. with 57. from 58. to 59. to 60. to 61. on 62. to.

EXERCISE 90

1. on 2. in 3. in 4. for 5. of 6. with 7. to 8. to 9. to 10. for 11. of 12. of 13. to 14. in 15. of 16. in 17. to 18. for 19. of 20. from 21. to 22. to 23. from 24. to 25. with 26. with 27. in 28. to 29. to 30. to 31. to 32. with 33. of 34. in 35. to 36. to 37. to 38. of 39. to 40. to 41. to 42. in 43. to 44. of 45. from 46. to 47. to 48. to 49. of 50. to.

EXERCISE 91

1. for, of 2. to 3. to, for 4. at, to 5. of, to 6. with, to 7. to, of 8. with, on 9. to, at, in 10. for, by 11. in, with 12. to, for 13. with, in 14. for , for 15. to, for 16. from, in 17. under, of 18. to, from 19. on, to 20. with, from 21. in, to 22. of, for/of 23. for, in, in 24. with for 25. of, on 26. with, of 27. to, to 28. to, on 29. with, for 30. for, to 31. in, to 32. on, to 33. from, with, through 34. from, to 35. of, for 36. to, of 37. by, by 38. to, of 39. with, from, to 40. to, beyond, with, to.

EXERCISE 92

1. from, between, for, by 2. from, for, for 3. against, of 4. for, of 5. in, of 6. about, with, in, at, for 7. from, with 8. from, on, under 9. to, in 10. to, with., among 11. from, with, of 12. upon, over, among 13. in, with, with 14. with, against, for 15. with, to 16. for, to, from 17. to, of 18. of, to 19. to, of, against 20. for, at , under .

EXERCISE 93

1. in, with, 2. about/of, about/of, to 3. in, for, with 4. for, of 5. over, for, of, on 6. to, of 7. for, of 8. from, to, with 9. with, to 10. at, with 11. on, with 12. with, by 13. with, to 14. for, in 15. with, in 16. to, for, at 17. in, of 18. to, for 19. of, in, from 20. with, on 21. to, for 22. for, with, to.

EXERCISE 94

1. unless—Subordinating	2. after—Subordinating
3. till—Subordinating	4. and—Co-ordinating
5. if—Subordinating	6. when—Subordinating
7. before—Subordinating	8. for—Co-ordinating
9. since—Subordinating	10. lest—Subordinating
11. if—Subordinating	12. before—Subordinating
13. after—Subordinating	14. because—Subordinating
15. than—Subordinating	16. before—subordinating
17. until—Subordinating	18. if—Subordinating
19. than—Subordinating	20. or—Co-ordinating
21. unless—Subordinating	22. whether—Subordinating
23. else— Co-ordinating	24. If—Subordinating
25. for—Co-ordinating	26. if—Subordinating
27. or—Co-ordinating	28. than—Subordinating
29. either...or—Co-ordinating	30. whether...or—Co-ordinating
31. unless— Subordinating	32. that— Subordinating
33. for—Co-ordinating	

================= **EXERCISE 95** =================

(1)   My brother smokes, *but* I don't.
       He must be *either* mad *or* drunk.
       Neither Mohan *nor* Padma is at home.
       I don't know *whether* he will come *or* not.
(2)   He told me *that* he would leave tomorrow.
       The train had departed *before* we reached the station.
       He asked *how* it had happened.
       You may do *as* you please.
       You can't catch the bus *unless* you run.
       I won't go away *until* you promise to help me.
       Though he studied hard, he failed the examination.
       I shall post your letters *when* I go out.
       While there is life, there is hope.
       I found my umbrella *where* I had left it.
       If it rains, we shall cancel the match.
       She is older *than* she looks.

================= **EXERCISE 96** =================

1. and 2. but 3. for 4. or/else/otherwise 5. Unless 6. that 7. till 8. till
9. though/although 10. lest 11. as/ because 12. As/Because 13. than
14. If 15. unless 16. than 17. as 18. If 19. so that 20. though/although
21. or 22. but 23. as/because 24. As

================= **EXERCISE 97** =================

1. and 2. or 3. if 4. Unless 5. yet 6. Until 7. for 8. as 9. that 10. when
11. though 12. till 13. but/and 14. and 15. but 16. or 17. and 18. as/when
19. if 20. as/because 21. so/and 22. but 23. and 24. but 25. or 26. but
27. but/and 28. as/because 29. unless 30. when/wherever/if 31. if 32. if
33. that 34. unless 35. If 36. till 37. and 38. whether 39. whether...or
40. while/when 41. since 42. as 43. that 44. neither...nor 45. than 46. Since
47. Since 48. Because 49. lest 50. that 51. While 52. till/until 53. that 54. since
55. though 56. so that 57. as/when/before/after 58. before 59. than 60. If
61.Though/ Although 62. Though/Although 63. where 64. when/wherever/if
65. as 66. as/because 67. Though/Although 68. that 69. if/whether
70. unless 71. unless 72. Though/Although 73. but 74. If 75. if 76. Though/
Although 77. since   78. lest 79. that 80. than

================= **EXERCISE 98** =================

1.   My brother is well, *but* my sister is ill.
2.   He sells mangoes *and* oranges.
3.   He did not succeed *though* he worked hard.

4. Rama *and* Hari played well.
5. I honour him *as/because* he is a brave man.
6. You may go, *but* I will stay.
7. Rama reads for pleasure, *but* Hari reads for profit.
8. We decided to set out *though* it was late.
9. He was poor *but* honest (or *Though* he was poor, he was honest).
10. He is *neither* a knave *nor* a fool.
11. We love Bahadur *as* he is a faithful dog.
12. Rustum made twelve runs *before* he was caught at the wicket.
13. He is rich *but* not happy. (*Though* rich, he is not happy)
14. The sheep *and* the oxen are grazing.
15. He is poor *but* contented. (*Though* he is poor, he is contented)
16. This mango is large *and* sweet.
17. *Neither* my brother *nor* my sister was there.
18. The boy *and* the girl are here.
19. The piper played *and/while* the children danced.
20. You must be quiet, *or* you must leave the room.
21. He sat down *as/because* he was tired.
22. Rama works hard *but* Hari is idle.
23. I lost the prize *though* I tried my best.
24. I like him *though* he is dangerous.
25. I went to the shop *and* bought a slate.
26. He is slow *but* sure.
27. I know *that* he does not think so.
28. You are tall, *but* my brother is taller. (or : My brother is taller *than* you.)
29. Hari went to school, *but/while* Sita stayed at home.
30. He must start at once, *or/else/otherwise* he will be late.
31. I shall sit still *and* listen to the music.
32. Hari *neither* came *nor* sent a letter.
33. I ran fast, *but* I missed the train. (or : *Though/Although* I ran fast I missed the train)
34. Karim works hard, *but* Abdul works harder. (or : Abdul works harder *than* Karim.)
35. He must be tired *as/because* he has walked five miles.
36. It is autumn, *so the leaves* are falling. (or : *As* it is autumn, the leaves are falling)
37. I will come *if* I am not ill.
38. I will bring your umbrella *if* you wish it.
39. He remained cheerful *though/although* he had been wounded
40. He went out *when/after* the rain stopped.
41. He ran to the station *but* missed the train.
42. I came, *though* unwilling.
43. Men have fought *and* died for their country.

44. He ran *lest* he should be late. (or : He ran *because/as* he was afraid of being late)

45. *Though/Although* Hari does not write fast, he writes very well. (or: Hari does not write fast, *but* he writes very well.)

46. The boy is dangerously ill *as* his head was hurt.

47. The old man fell down the steps *and* broke his leg.

48. He tried to get up, *but* could not.

49. *Both* mother and father are at home.

50. I have a cricket bat *and* a set of stumps.

51. *Though/Although* we went early to the circus, we could not get a seat. (or : We went early to the circus *but* could not get a seat.)

52. He must do *as* he is told, *or /else/otherwise* he will be punished.

53. The prisoner fell down on his knees *and* begged for mercy.

54. *Both* Sita *and* Ganga go to school.

55. Rama may be *either* in the house *or* in garden.

EXERCISE 99

1. Preposition 2. Adverb 3. Conjunction 4. Adverb 5. Preposition 6. Conjunction 7. Adverb 8. Preposition 9. Conjection 10. Conjunction 11. Preposition 12. Adverb

EXERCISE 100

1. but 2. yet 3. and 4. where 5. but 6. and 7. when 8. either...or 9. neither...nor 10. so 11. for 12. while 13. but 14. but 15. when 16. though/although 17. and 18. but 19. but 20. than 21. that 22. but 23. but 24. than 25. Though/Although, yet 26. than 27. when 28. but 29. but 30. though/although 31. but 32. or 33. and 34. and 35. when 36. and 37. except 38. though/although 39. when 40. neither...nor 41. not only...but 42. but 43. and,as 44. and 45. but 46. though/although 47. that 48. unless 49. though/although 50. if

EXERCISE 101

1. Though 2. but 3. until/till 4. when, and 5. but 6. unless 7. when 8. that, than 9. for 10. that 11. but, than 12. but 13. but, but 14. and 15. but 16. than 17. when 18. when, than 19. and 20. when, and, when, and 21. if 22. but 23. though 24. If 25. when, and, neither...nor 26. except 27. than 28. than, yet 29. than 30. but 31. and 32. than 33. either...or 34. but 35. while 36. when, 37. If 38. for 39. but 40. and 41. when 42. but 43. than 44. for 45. Though, yet 46. and 47. while 48. if 49. either...or 50. until 51. or, but.

EXERCISE 102

1. Noun 2. Verb 3. Adjective 4. Noun 5. Adjective 6. Adjective 7. Adverb 8. Adjective 9. Adverb 10. Adjective 11. Adverb 12. Adverb 13. Adverb 14. Noun 15. Adjective 16. Adverb 17. Adjective 18. Adverb 19. Adjective 20. Adverb 21. Adjective 22. Adverb 23. Adjective 24. Adverb 25. Adverb 26. Pronoun 27. Adverb 28. Adjective 29. Adverb 30. Adverb 31. Preposition 32. Preposition 33. Adverb 34. Adverb 35. Preposition 36. Adverb 37. Adverb 38. Preposition 39. Adjective 40. Conjunction 41. Adverb 42. Conjunction 43. Adjective 44. Pronoun 45. Adverb 46. Pronoun 47. Adjective 48. Pronoun 49. Adverb 50. Pronoun.

EXERCISE 103

1. Adverb 2. Adjective 3. Adverb 4. Conjunction 5. Conjunction 6. Conjunction 7. Conjunction 8. Conjunction 9. Noun 10. Adverb 11. Adjective 12. Adverb 13. Preposition 14. Preposition 15. Adverb 16. Preposition 17. Conjunction 18. Relative Pronoun 19. Preposition 20. Noun 21. Adverb 22. Noun 23. Adjective 24. Preposition 25. Verb 26. Noun 27. Preposition 28. Pronoun 29. Adverb 30. Pronoun 31. Preposition 32. Adjective 33. Adverb 34. Adjective 35. Adverbs 36. Noun 37. Verb 38. Noun 39. Adjective 40. Adjective 41. Adjective 42. Conjunction 43. Preposition 44. Adverb 45. Adjective 46. Conjunction 47. Relative Pronoun 48. Relative Pronoun 49. Adjective 50. Pronoun.

BOOK II – COMPOSITION

EXERCISE 1

1. The cackling of geese —Subject
   saved Rome—Predicate
2. Stone walls—Subject
   do not a prison make—Predicate
3. All matter—Subject
   is indestructible—Predicate
4. No man—Subject
   can serve two masters—Predicate
5. A sick room—Subject
   should be well aired—Predicate
6. I—Subject
   shot an arrow in the air—Predicate
7. the shepherd—Subject
   A barking sound...hears—Predicate
8. the balloon—Subject
   Up went—Predicate
9. he—Subject
   The naked every day...clad—Predicate
10. the piper—Subject
    Into the street...stepped—Predicate
11. the uses of adversity—Subject
    Sweet are—Predicate
12. Dear, gentle, patient, noble Nell—Subject
    was dead—Predicate

EXERCISE 2

Sentence	Complete Subject	Subject word	Its Attributes
1.	The boy, anxious to learn	boy	The anxious to learn
2.	A burnt child	child	A burnt
3.	Birds of a feather	Birds	of a feather
4.	The attempt to scale the fort	attempt	The, to scale the fort
5.	The days of our youth	days	The, of our youth
6.	Ill habits	habits	Ill
7.	The dog, seizing the man by the collar	dog	The, seizing the man by the collar
8.	The streets of some of our cities	streets	The, of some of our cities
9.	A house divided against itself	house	A, divided against itself
10.	Deceived by his friends, he	he	Deceived by his friends

53

11.	One man carrying a hoe	man	The, carrying a hoe
12.	One man's meat	meat	One man's
13.	My days among the dead	days	My, among the dead
14.	the stout old sheriff	sheriff	the stout old

EXERCISE 3

1. distinctly—Adverb
2. in a distinct voice—Adverbial phrase
3. a mile—Adverbial Accusative
4. again—Adverb
5. to stay—Gerundial Infinitive
6. a minute—Adverbial Accusative
7. in clear type—Adverbial phrase
8. at once—Adverbial phrase
9. over a stile—Adverbial phrase
10. The tide having turned—Absolute phrase
11. below its value—Adverbial phrase
12. behind him—Adverbial phrase
13. by painting—Adverbial phrase
14. by trade—Adverbial phrase
15. inch by inch—Adverbial phrase
16. about him—Adverbial phrase
17. in all respects—Adverbial phrase
18. to the ends of the earth—Adverbial phrase

EXERCISE 4

1. a soldier—Noun
2. sweet—Adjective
3. pleased—Adjective
4. tired—Adjective
5. round—Adjective
6. happy—Adjective
7. sweet—Adjective
8. dead—Adjective
9. cold—Adjective
10. unconscious—Adjective
11. of a gentle disposition—Adjectival Phrase
12. there—Adverb
13. health—Adjective
14. sad—Adjective
15. full to the brim—Adjectival Phrase
16. shocking—Adjectival
17. of the modern athlete—Adjectival Phrase
18. about—Adverb
19. the pride of the village—Noun Phrase
20. in good spirits—Adjectival Phrase
21. lending to the lord—Noun Phrase
22. of considerable importance—Adjectival Phrase
23. the architect of his own fortune—Noun Phrase

EXERCISE 5

Sentence	Complete Subject	Object-word	Its Attributes
1.	nothing of its greatest men	nothing	of its greatest men
2.	to govern ourselves	to govern	ourselves
3.	her arms	arms	her
4.	a plan for the house	plan	a, for the house
5.	their skin	skin	their
6.	the wind	wind	the
7.	them	them	......
8.	the baby	baby	the
9.	his master's confidence	confidence	his master's
10.	your voice	voice	your
11.	your coat	coat	your
12.	houses	houses	......
13.	no answer to my letter	answer	no, to my letter
14.	the knell of parting day	knell	the, of parting day
15.	the heat of the sun	heat	the, of the sun
16.	good manners	manners	good

EXERCISE 6

Sentence	Subject	Predicate		
		Verb	Object	Complement
1.	Abdul	called	his cousin	a fool
2.	Exercise	has made	his muscles	strong
3.	This	will make	you	happy
4.	The Nawab	appointed	his own brother	Vizier
5.	The court	appointed	him	guardian of the orphan child
6.	Time	makes	the worst enemies	friends
7.	Sickness	made	the child	irritable
8.	They	elected	him	secretary of the club
9.	You	do take	me	for a fool
10.	We	saw	the storm	approaching
11.	I	consider	the man	trustworthy
12.	They	kept	us	in suspense
13.	The jury	found	him	guilty of murder
14.	A thunderstorm	(often) turns	milk	sour

EXERCISE 20

No.	SUBJECT		Verb	PREDICATE		
	Subject-word	Attribute		Object	Complement	Adverbial Qualification
1.	nod	(1) A (2) From a lord	is	...	breakfast for a fool	...
2.	paymaster	(1) A (2) good	wants	...	workmen	never
3.	they	...	brought	her warrior	dead	home
4.	Sickness	...	made	the child	irritable	...
5.	Evangeline	Gentle	was	...	the pride of the village	...
6.	(It) to find fault	...	is	...	easy	...
7.	(It) to live in suspense	...	is	...	a miserable thing	...
8.	Wounds	made by words	are	...	hard to heal	...
9.	George	(1) the (2) royal	went	...	...	down

| No. | SUBJECT | | Verb | PREDICATE | | |
	Subject-word	Attribute		Object	Complement Qualification	Adverbial
10.	hundred	(1) the (2) six	rode	...	... valley of death	into the
11.	Time	...	makes	the worst enemies	friends	...
12.	reward	(1) your (2) in heaven	is	...	Great	...
13.	India	...	loat	a true friend	...	in him
14.	proof	(1) the (2) of the pudding	is	...	in the eating	...
15.	(It) to be wise	after the event	is	...	easy	...
16.	he	...	was	the country dear	A man to all	...
17.	Experience	...	has taught	(1) us (2) many lessons	...	...

No.	SUBJECT		PREDICATE			
	Subject-word	Attribute	Verb	Object	Complement	Adverbial Qualification
18.	Care	(1) A man's (2) first	should be	...	to avoid the reproaches of his own heart	...
19.	work and play	(1) all (2) no	makes	Jack	a dull boy	...
20.	He	...	showed	a constant solicitude for his son's welfare	...	...
21.	Caesar	...	returned	...	...	(1) having conquered his enemies (2) to Rome
22.	To drive	a motor-car	requires	care and skill	...	...
23.	fortune	(1) a (2) great (3) in the hands of a fool	is	...	a great mis-fortune	...
24.	postman	The	looked	... day	very tired	at the end of the

EXERCISE 8

1. in great difficulties
2. of very considerable renown
3. in small cages
4. without any enemy; with few friends
5. with the ring of truth in it
6. in need
7. in time
8. in the hand; in the bush
9. with cool shady trees
10. with plenty of money; of such beauty and power
11. of his cruel wrongs
12. of the noble Padmini
13. of great promise
14. with a strange device
15. of one of the criminal tribes.

EXERCISE 9

1. A *grey* cloud— A cloud *of grey colour*
2. a *wooden* hut—a hut *built of wood*
3. a *bald head*—a head *without (much) hair* (or : *in a bald state*)
4. a *diamond* necklace—a necklace *set with diamonds*
5. a *horrible* night—a night *full of horror*
6. the *Siberian* railways—the railway *running through Siberia*
7. A *grassy* meadow—A meadow *covered with grass*
8. An *earthen* pitcher—A pitcher *made of earth*
   a *three-legged* table—a table *with three legs*
9. The French flag—The flag of France.
   the *highest* mast—the mast *of the greatest height*
10. a *cowardly* act—an act *of cowardice*
11. *well*—in good health
12. A *valuable* ring—A ring *of value.*
13. *Heroic* deeds—deeds *of heroism*
14. the *Swiss* scenery—secenery *of Switzerland*
15. *Numerical* superiority—superiority *in numbers*
16. *material* glory—glory *in matter.*
17. *sleepless* nights—nights *without sleep*
18. *a professional* cricketer—a cricketer *by profession*
19. *biblical* quotations—quotations *from the Bible*
20. *medical* advice— advice *of a medical nature*
21. *a tall* soldier—a soldier *of a tall stature*

EXERCISE 10

1. a turban *made of silk*—a *silk* turban
2. a deed *of shame*—a *shameful* deed
3. a life *devoid of blame*—a *blameless* life
4. a man *without a friend*—a *friendless* man
5. a path *covered with mud*—a *muddy* path
6. a sword *stained with blood*—a *blood-stained* sword
7. a girl *from a cottage*—a *cottage* girl

8. a man *with plenty of impudence*—an *impudent* man
9. this village *in the mountains*—this *mountainous* village
10. a soldier *full of hope* and *free from fear*—a *hopeful* and *fearless* soldier
11. a boy *without fear*—a *fearless* boy
12. a person *with a bad temper*—a *bad-tempered* person
13. a man *of sense*—a *sensible* man
14. The tops *of the mountains*—The *mountain* tops
15. an author *of great versatility*—a *versatile* author
16. *of no use*—useless

EXERCISE 11

1. with a white skin
2. of the same feather
3. of simplicity
4. with pictures
5. of great value
6. full of wisdom
7. of great prudence
8. of renown
9. of your school
10. of this tree
11. of voices
12. of the cuckoo
13. of the jury
14. of the office
15. of the canal
16. leading to the church
17. of that hotel
18. of glory

EXERCISE 12

1. He is a man *of great talent*.
2. The result *of the debate* is not known.
3. Mohan loves a girl *with blue eyes*.
4. Childhood is a period *of rapid growth*.
5. I have bought a car *of British make*.

EXERCISE 13

1. in the middle of a great wood 2. on the moon 3. into the garden 4. over the sea 5. O'er her 6. Down in a green and shady bed 7. On your conscience 8. for a while, on the bank of the river 9. on his face 10. with a loud report 11. beside the river Dee 12. on the bridge; at midnight 13. To the northward 14. Beside a green meadow 15. to my great profit 16. in her ear 17. Beside the ungathered rice. 18. to the last man 19. in the face of all obstacles 20. on my toe 21. at arm's length 22. at home 23. at any price 24. at a fearful rate 25. in his proper colours 26. on the pulse of the nation 27. by his pen 28. at the top of his voice 29. with all his might 30. Without pausing to consider 31. under the bridge; since then

EXERCISE 14

1. with swiftness 2. in a good manner 3. to a distance 4. in a feeble voice 5. in a gentle manner 6. in this place 7. in a short time 8. in that place 9. a short time

ago 10. with cheer 11. with eloquence 12. in a short time 13. in a thorough manner 14. towards home 15. in a suspicious way 16. from that time onward 17. with all his might

EXERCISE 15

1. terribly 2. henceforth 3. here 4. truthfully 5. then 6. soon 7. promptly 8. impudently 9. unreservedly 10. heartily 11. ultimately 12. proverbially 13. fiercely 14. properly 15. violently 16. satisfactorily

EXERCISE 16

1. with great courage
2. with respect
3. with his axe
4. at random
5. to please my father
6. in a reckless manner
7. in haste
8. with contempt
9. with care
10. with caution
11. two years ago
12. on time
13. with diligence
14. in the examination
15. to bed

EXERCISE 17

1. Are you going *to the cinema*?
2. *In all probability* he will arrive tonight.
3. I shall return the book in *a couple of days*.
4. I see him *every day*.
5. *In spite of his hard work,* he did not succeed.

EXERCISE 18

1. Adjective Phrase
2. Adverb Phrase
3. Adverb Phrase
4. Adjective Phrase
5. Adjective Phrase
6. Adverb Phrase
7. Adjective Phrase
8. Adverb Phrase

EXERCISE 19

She usually speaks *in a loud voice*.
Please send the articles *without further delay*.
All the people supported the Government's policy *with one voice*.
I cannot say *for certain* when I shall be back.
We were *just in time* for the train.
The workers are *up in arms against* the manager.
What he says is *of no consequence*.
The style of dress has *gone out of fashion*.
She accepted the gift *with great satisfaction*.
He left in the *twinkling of an eye*.
There are trees *on either side of the street*.

They were relaxing *in a shady nook.*
They were killed *to the last man.*
He accepted the challenge *with a smile.*
In his house everything is *at sixes and sevens.*
He offered to join in the game *at the eleventh hour.*
Standing *on the top of the hill,* I saw the whole town.
Behave well *in future.*
He asked me to meet him at *nine o'clock.*

EXERCISE 20

1. to speak to the Headmaster 2. getting people into trouble 3. to pay back every penny of the money 4. having to punish his servants 5. living in darkness 6. to do such a thing 7. climbing a coconut palm 8. thinking good thoughts 9. to answer the question 10. to write such rubbish 11. to come again 12. visiting such a man 13. Travelling in a hot dusty train 14. stealing the money 15. Your doing such a thing.

EXERCISE 21

1. I want *to visit the museum.*
2. *Swimming across the river* delights me.
3. We all hope *to see you soon.*
4. Pretend *to know nothing about it.*
5. *To behave like that* seems dishonest.
6. *My getting a first class* surprised my mother.
7. Do you wish *to go home*?
8. My father hates *playing cards.*
9. *Going to the movies* gives me no pleasure.
10. I don't intend *to harm you.*
11. *To give up smoking* is not easy.
12. I do not expect *to finish the work today.*
13. I enjoy *reading detective stories.*
14. He wishes *to go into business.*
15. Cats like *catching mice.*
16. His father promised *to send him abroad.*

EXERCISE 22

1. like a born orator—Adverb Phrase
2. to hear of your illness—Noun Phrase
3. Beyond a doubt—Adverb Phrase
4. in spite of his best efforts—Adverb Phrase
5. by means of trickery—Adverb Phrase
6. like that—Adverb Phrase
7. how to play this game—Noun Phrase

8. in spite of many faults—Adverb Phrase
9. at your hands—Adverb Phrase
10. to be understood—Adverb Phrase
11. what to do—Noun Phrase
12. how to solve this problem—Noun Phrase
13. amidst many difficulties—Adverb Phrase
14. in the long run—Adverb Phrase
15. of a feather—Adjective Phrase
16. of no importance—Adjective Phrase
17. behind time—Adverb Phrase
18. of means—Adjective Phrase
19. near his heart—Adverb Phrase
20. under lock and key—Adverb Phrase
21. of no importance—Adjective Phrase
22. to go to the cinema today—Noun Phrase
23. to hear the watch-dog's honest bark—Noun Phrase
24. of my own free will—Adverb Phrase
25. how to do it—Noun Phrase
26. over a dog—Adverb Phrase
27. in a bad way—Adverb Phrase
28. of wonderful patience—Adjective Phrase
29. to his secret—Adjective Phrase
30. of committing us to nothing—Adjective Phrase
31. of the story—Adjective Phrase
32. How to find the way to the ruins—Noun Phrase
33. of might—Adjective Phrase
34. against his will—Adverb Phrase
35. to waste on trifles—Adjective Phrase
36. by halves—Adverb Phrase
37. walking in the fields—Noun Phrase

EXERCISE 23

1. wherever you like 2. where his pursuers could not follow 3. as one might expect him to do. 4. Because you have done this 5. As he was not there 6. If you eat too much 7. though he began late 8. till I return 9. Just as he entered the room 10. where living was cheaper 11. as he thinks 12. because the night is dark 13. because I choose to 14. If I make a promise 15. if you work hard 16. as far as he dared 17. since you repent 18. where I am 19. until you come 20. When I was younger 21. that you could not see your hand 22. Wherever one goes 23. If you do not hurry 24. Since you have already decided.

EXERCISE 24

1. till the rain stops **2.** as you are **3.** that I didn't mind the consequences **4.** that I failed to catch him **5.** as I tell him **6.** that we could not hear him **7.** if you scold me **8.** where wise men fear to tread **9.** because he is arrogant **10.** than secret love (is) **11.** if he works hard **12.** while the sun shines **13.** that he cannot attend the meeting **14.** unless I telephone you **15.** when his father was asleep **16.** as I advise him **17.** if I call him **18.** as he was ordered **19.** as her mother does **20.** than the moon (is) **21.** before he was born **22.** unless he wears glasses **23.** so that you may please your boss **24.** where I had left them **25.** if it rains **26.** according to what is deserved **27.** than geometry (is) **28.** if we don't take a taxi **29.** as you please.

EXERCISE 25

1. on his return— When he returned
2. to the best of your ability—as well as you can.
3. on his arrival—when he arrived
4. in spite of his poverty—though he was poor
5. upon seeing the signal—when they saw the signal
6. without hard work—unless he works hard
7. for his kindness—because he was kind
8. in comparison with air—When it is compared with air
9. too bright to last—so bright that it cannot last
10. (too full) for words—(so full) that I cannot express my feelings in words
11. (too much) for any man to do single-handed—so much that no man can do it single-handed
12. With a view to early retirement—that he might retire early
13. In the event of the president's death—If the president dies
14. according to instructions—as he was instructed
15. for an old car—as it is an old car
16. with all his might—as fast as he could
17. after such hard work—As he has done such hard work
18. (base enough) to accept the dishonourable terms—(so base) that he accepted the dishonourable terms.
19. as to be wholly unmanageable—that they were wholly unmanageable
20. by any other name—even if it were called by any other name

EXERCISE 26

1. since I returned from Madras—since my return from Madras
2. When the sun set—At sunset (or : The sun having set)
3. as heroes do—like heroes (or : heroically)
4. when the righteous rule—Under the rule of the righteous
5. Though I am poor—In spite of my poverty

6. that we may help you—to help you
7. When he entered the room—(On) entering the room
8. as a jackal does—like a jackal
9. that he has recovered from his illness—of his recovery from his illness
10. that he may become rich—to become rich
11. that he succeeded—as to succeed
12. As soon as I saw the cobra—Immediately on seeing the cobra
13. that we might arrive in time—so as to arrive in time
14. even as he lay dying—even on his death bed
15. unless he applies himself continually to his art—without applying himself continually to his art
16. if only he might make profit—to make profit
17. (so rich) that he could buy a motor-car— (rich enough) to buy a motor car
18. when he had uttered these words—After uttering these words
19. (so difficult) that I cannot do it—too difficult for me to do
20. (so good) that it cannot be true— (too good) to be true
21. As I had no money with me — having no money with me
22. that he might live long— so as to live long
23. as soon as the mails arrive— on the arrival of the mails
24. after his work finished—after finishing his work
25. As he was sick— Being sick
26. as he deserved— deservedly
27. so far as the working is concerned— in respect of working
28. that the streets were flooded— as to flood the streets
29. because you recommended him—because of your recommendation
30. though they were of noble birth— in spite of their noble birth
31. whatever I may say— for all my admonition
32. as well as we can— to the best of our ability
33. when he discovered the print of a foot on the sand— at the discovery of the print of a foot on the sand
34. as long as the Roman Empire lasted— throughout the period of the Roman Empire
35. though his income was only £40 annually— in spite of his income being only £ 40 annually
36. because you are kind to us— because of your kindness to us
37. (so difficult) that I cannot comprehend it— (too difficult) for me to comprehend

EXERCISE 27

1. whose fleece was white as snow— qualifies 'lamb'
2. which was badly needed— qualifies — 'money '
3. that I live in— qualifies 'house'

4.   (that) I survey— qualifies 'all '
5.   which goes in and out with me— qualifies 'shadow'
6.   that bites— qualifies 'dog'
7.   that sounds untrue— qualifies 'tale'
8.   that blows nobody any good— qualifies 'wind'
9.   whence all but he had fled — qualifies 'deck'
10. who die in great cause— qualifies 'they'
11. where I was born— qualifies 'house'
12. that climbs too high — qualifies 'he'
13. (that) you want— qualifies 'book'
14. who help themselves— qualifies 'those'
15. where he was born— qualifies 'village'
16. that is silly— qualifies 'anything'
17. who live in glass houses—qualifies 'people'
18. that has no turning— qualifies 'lane'
19. who laughs last— qualifies 'he'
20. that hath his quarrel just— qualifies 'he'

EXERCISE 28

1. where he lives 2. who is true to his word 3. which he is referring to
4. which cannot be excused 5. which I borrowed from the library 6. who have
failed in more than two subjects 7. that he bought yesterday 8. that I had lost
9. who beat your brother 10. who is honest 11. who is standing there 12. where
I had left it 13. where pearl oysters are abundant 14. which is meant for
drinking 15. who comes late 16. which departed at 8:30

EXERCISE 29

1.   of industrious habits— who is of industrious habits
2.   the time of his arrival— when he would arrive (or : when he had ar-
     rived)
3.   for departing— when he is to depart
4.   leading to the temple— which leads to the temple
5.   filled with almonds— which is filled with almonds
6.   of courage— who is courageous
7.   on a hill— which is situated on a hill
8.   in the gallery— who were sitting in the gallery
9.   of your liking— that you like
10. of the Burmans— in which the Burmans live

═══ EXERCISE 30 ═══

1. in which Burmans live— of the Burmese
2. who sits near me— sitting near me
3. why he came late— for his coming late
4. why he failed— for his failure
5. who were weary with their exertions— being weary with their exertions
6. which at midday was hot— being hot at midday.
7. that leads most quickly to the station— leading most quickly to the station
8. who eat too much— eating too much
9. who have not been trained to write— not trained to write
10. where our forefathers landed— of landing of our forefathers
11. (that) he gave— given by him
12. (Such men) as you (are)— Men like you
13. (This boy) who is industrious— The industrious boy
14. (A belief) which is generally held— A generally held belief
15. who was famous in the reign of Queen Anne— famous in the reign of Queen Anne
16. which overlooks the lake— overlooking the lake

═══ EXERCISE 31 ═══

1. how you are getting on 2. that I shall fail 3. that he would come 4. that you stole the watch 5. that it would be a fine day 6. that you should cheat me 7. who he is 8. that the clock had stopped 9. That you should say this 10. how you can get out of this much 11. whatever I can 12. what he wants 13. that the day was hot 14. what had happened 15. how it all hapened 16. what I am going to say 17. that she was ill 18. how far it is from here 19. Where we were to lodge that night 20. that his life might be spared 21. (that) you have made a mistake 22. what I want 23. How the burglar got in 24. whether he will come 25. what he will do

═══ EXERCISE 32 ═══

1. why he robbed his friend 2. that they wished to go for a picnic 3. that he is European 4. what I wanted 5. that they had deceived him 6. That he is a smuggler 7. where he lives 8. what she wants 9. who he is 10. how the machine operates 11. That we shall win the match 12. that you will win the scholarship 13. that I am busy 14. when the next train will arrive 15. that his son should study medicine 16. that you owe me Rs. 10 17. that he will get a first class 18. that he is going to the United States ? 19. Whatever you do 20. what I had done

═══ EXERCISE 33 ═══

1. When he will come 2. that he had succeeded 3. Why he failed 4. that the weather will change 5. that the man was guilty 6. that business will improve 7. that his statement is true 8. that he is trustworthy 9. what he has said 10. that

he was guilty **11.** how they attacked the camp **12.** Where they met **13.** where the wind was blowing from **14.** that he would arrive **15.** that he would succeed **16.** that you have great regard for him.

EXERCISE 34

1. that I shall be there in time— to be there in time
2. that we will win the match— of our winning the match
3. that it was a fine day— upon the fine day
4. where he is concealed— the place of his concealment
5. where he is going— his residence
6. that the man is sincere— (the man) to be sincere
7. what you think about this— your opinion of this
8. that she will soon recover— of her recovery
9. (It is to be regretted) that he retired from the world so early in life— His retirement from the world so early in life (is to be regretted)
10. what he says—his words (or : him)
11. how the problem was done—the method of doing the problem
12. (It seems) that he is a sharper—(He seems) to be a sharper
13. where I live—my residence
14. why you did this—the reason for doing this
15. (It is not known) who has written this book—The author of this book (is not known)
16. whosoever is guilty —the guilty

EXERCISE 35

1. When you like —Adverb Clause, modifying **'come'**
2. who is here—Adjective Clause, qualifying **'book'**
3. that he met your brother—Noun Clause, object of —**'says'**
4. that rocks the cradle—Adjective Clause, qualifying **'hand'**
5. Before I die—Adverb Clause, modifying **'intend'**
6. as we go forward—Adverb Clause, modifying **'rejoice'**
7. Which I had heard before—Adjective Clause, qualifying **'book'**
8. that I am a fool—Noun Clause, object of **'thinks'**
9. As I drew near—Adverb Clause, modifying **'saw'**
10. whom I knew—Adjective Clause, qualifying **'friends'**
11. whose soul is dead—Adjective Clause, qualifying **'man'**
12. that he will die—Noun clause, object of **'thinks'**
13. who did this—Adjective Clause, qualifying **'man'**
14. that he would fast for a week—Noun Clause, put in apposition to **'vow'**
15. that Rama has won the prize—Noun Clause, object of **'have heard'**
16. whom the king suspected—Adjective Clause, qualifying **'vizier'**
17. that he wrote the letter—Noun Clause, object of **'admitted'**
18. That he will do it—Noun Clause, referring to **'doubt'**

19. which you mention—Adjective Clause, qualifying **'place'**
20. That such a thing could happen—Noun Clause, object of **'do not believe'**
21. When he heard this—Adverb Clause, modifying **'turned'**
22. that he has bought—Adjective Clause, qualifying **'horse'**
23. that you will visit us—Noun Clause, object of **'hopes'**
24. as a brave man should do—Adverb Clause, modifying **'behaved'**
25. until the next train comes—Adverb Clause, modifying **'will wait'**
26. that he would be surrounded—Noun Clause, object of **'feared'**
27. when he was hungry—Adverb Clause, modifying **'ate'**
28. Since he has been in hospital—Adverb Clause, modifying **'has improved'**
29. As I was going in—Adverb Clause, modifying **'came'**
30. when he was tired of waiting—Noun Clause, put in apposition to **'time'**
31. when wars should cease—Noun Clause, put in apposition with **'time'**
32. where the climate is good—Adverb Clause, modifying **'live'**
33. where roses grow—Adjective Clause, qualifying **'place'**
34. whither few travellers go—Adjective Clause, qualifying **'land'**
35. whither it listeth—Adverb Clause, modifying **'bloweth'**
36. whence they had come—Adverb Clause, modifying **'returned'**
37. whence such birds migrate—Adjective Clause, qualifying **'coun- try'**
38. whither I now depart—Adjective Clause, qualifying **'retreat'**
39. when the monsoon failed—Noun Clause, put in apposition with **'year'**
40. where you'll get rich in a hurry—Adjective Clause, qualifying **'place'**
41. whence they had so hopefully set forth that morning—Adjective Clause, qualifying **'prison'**
42. when you did this—Adjective Clause, qualifying **'day'**
43. where once I sat—Adjective Clause, qualifying **'seat'**
44. whence no traveller returns—Adjective Clause, qualifying **'bourne'**

■ EXERCISE 36 ■

1. where he can sleep—Adjective Clause
2. who has long hair—Adjective Clause
3. what the news is—Noun Clause
4. Though he has made efforts—Adverb Clause
5. (so) that he might avoid slipping—Adverb Clause
6. where I live—Noun Clause
7. as he was full of joy—Adverb Clause
8. what you have asked —Noun Clause
9. (so) that he may earn his livelihood—Adverb Clause
10. As he is lame—Adverb Clause
11. When the sun set—Adverb Clause
12. that he had arrived—Noun Clause
13. How long the war will last—Noun Clause

14. What he had remarked (was)—Noun Clause
15. that he was innocent—Noun Clause
16. that he will recover soon—Noun Clause
17. why he had come—Noun Clause
18. that the traitor (should) be executed—Noun Clause
19. that the boy was impudent—Noun Clause
20. That he is silent—Noun Clause
21. when I shall arrive—Noun Clause
22. That he had a share in the plot—Noun Clause
23. as a born orator does—Adverb Clause
24. As existing conditions are such—Adverb Clause
25. that he will accept your offer—Adverb Clause
26. Where I lived before—Adverb Clause
27. if you behave well—Adverb Clause

EXERCISE 37

1. Compound Sentence
   (i) The horse reared (ii) the rider was thrown ('and')
2. Compound Sentence
   (i) Walk quickly (ii) you will not overtake him ('else')
3. Complex Sentence
   (i) The town is very large (Main Clause) (ii) in which I live (Adjective Clause)
4. Compound Sentence
   (i) I called him (ii) he gave me no answer ('but')
5. Compound Sentence
   (i) I agree to your proposals (ii) I think them reasonable ('for')
6. Complex Sentence
   (i) I went (Main Clause) (ii) because I was invited (Adverb Clause)
7. Compound Sentence
   (i) he is drowned (ii) some passing ship has saved him ('Either...or')
8. Complex Sentence
   (i) I returned home (Main Clause) (ii) because I was tired (Adverb Clause)
9. Complex Sentence
   (i) They always talk (Main Clause) (ii) who never think (Adjective clause)
10. Complex Sentence
    (i) He came oftener (Main Clause) (ii) than we expected (Adverb Clause)
11. Compound Sentence
    (i) He blushes (ii) he is guilty ('therefore')
12. Complex Sentence
    (i) A guest is unwelcome (Main Clause) (ii) when he stays too long (Adverb clause)

13. Complex Sentence
    (i) Do well (Main Clause) (ii) whatever you do (North Clause)
14. Compound Sentence
    (i) He must have done his duty (ii) he is conscientious man ('for')
15. Compound Sentence
    (i) He rushed into the field (ii) foremost fighting fell ('and')
16. Compound Sentence
    (i) Man proposes (ii) God disposes ('but')
17. Complex Sentence
    (i) 'tis folly to be wise (Main Clause) (ii) where ignorance is bliss
    (Adverb Clause)
18. Compound Sentence
    (i) Listen carefully (ii) take notes ('and')
19. Compound Sentence
    (i) The heavens declare the glory of God (ii) the firmament showeth
    his handiwork ('and')
20. Compound Sentence
    (i) He tried hard (ii) he did not succeed ('but')
21. Compound Sentence
    (i) She must weep (ii) she will die ('or')
22. Complex Sentence
    (i) They serve God well (Main Clause) (ii) who serve His creatures
    (Adjective Clause)
23. Compound Sentence
    (i) Man is guided by reason (ii) beasts (are guided) by instinct ('and')
24.   Complex Sentence
    (i) Quarrels would not last long (Main Clause) (ii) if the fault were
    only on one side (Adverb Clause)
25. Compound Sentence
    (i) God made the country (ii) man made the town ('and')
26. Complex Sentence
    (i) He trudged on (Main Clause) (ii) though he was very tired
    (Adverb Clause)
27. Complex Sentence
    (i) There was one philosopher (Main Clause) (ii) who chose to live in a
    tub (Adjective Clause)
28. Compound Sentence
    (i) The Commons passed the bill (ii) the Lords threw it out ('but')
29. Compound Sentence
    (i) Tell me the news (Main Clause) (ii) as you have heard (Adverb Clause)
30. Complex Sentence
    (i) He has none to lose (Main Clause) (ii) that has most time (Adjective
    Clause)

31. Compound Sentence
    (i) Your arguments are weighty (ii) they do not convince me (**'still'**)
32. Complex Sentence
    (i) Everything comes (Main Clause) (ii) if a man will only work and wait (Adverb Clause)
33. Compound Sentence
    (i) The same day went Jesus out of the house (ii) (he) sat by the sea-side (**'and'**)
34. Compound Sentence
    (i) We must eat to live (ii) we should not live to eat (**'but'**)
35. Compound Sentence
    (i) Govern your passions (ii) they will govern you (**'or'**)
36. Compound Sentence
    (i) They fought the dogs (ii) (they) killed the cats (iii) (they) bit the babies in the cradles (iv) (they) ate the cheeses out of the vats (v) licked the soup from the cook's own ladles (**'and'...**)
37. Complex Sentence
    (i) My heart leaps up (Main Clause) (ii) when I behold a rainbow in the sky (Adverb Clause)

EXERCISE 38

(i) **As subject of a verb:**
    Whether he will come at all is doubtful.
    What she said may be true.
    Whoever finishes first gets a prize.

(ii) **As object of a verb:**
    He said *that he had not heard the news.*
    I don't know *where he has gone.*
    I doubt *whether he will accept the offer.*

(iii) **In apposition to a noun or pronoun :**
    We must allow for the fact *that she doesn't hear well.*
    Never forget this, *that a stitch* in time saves nine.
    It is unfortunate *that you have lost your purse.*

(iv) **As complement of a verb :**
    My belief is *that he is innocent.*
    The truth is *that they are married.*
    My request is *that I may be allowed to go now.*

EXERCISE 39

1. how you found that out —object of the verb **'tell'**
2. That he will succeed—subject of the verb **'is'**
3. (that) you have made a mistake—object of the verb **'think'**

4. (that) her mother is ill—object of the verb **'says'**
5. How long I shall stay here—subject of the verb **'is'**
6. that he had come—object of the verb **'did (not) know'**
7. that he was guilty—put in apposition to the pronoun **'It'**
8. how it all happened—object of the verb **'do (not) understand'**
9. who wrote *Shakuntala*—object of the verb **'can tell'**
10. how it is done—object of the preposition **'on'**
11. that you stole the purse—object of the verb **'do deny'**
12. whosoever is guilty—object of the verb **'will punish'**
13. (that) I know your face—object of the verb **'know'**
14. if dinner is ready—object of the verb **'ask'**
15. that he was killed—put in apposition to the noun **'report'**
16. that he would succeed —connected with the adjective **'hopeful'**
17. whatever you think right—object of the verb **'do'**
18. how can you get out of this mess—object of the verb **'don't see'**
19. when the train will arrive—object of the verb **'Do know'**
20. whoever came—subject of the verb **'was'**
21. (that) you want a situation—object of the verb **'understand'**
22. that the prisoners shall die—complement of the verb **'is'**
23. how sorry I am—object of the verb **'cannot express'**
24. what he meant—object of the verb **'guessed'**
25. that she will be angry—connected with the adjective **'afraid'**
26. why you behaved so—object of the verb **'will explain'**
27. how this will end—object of the verb **'can tell'**
28. that we have been deceived—complement of the verb **'is'**
29. who has done this—put is apposition to the pronoun **'It'**
30. how I can deal with this rascal—object of the verb **'do (not) know'**
31. whether I should laugh or cry—object of the verb **'did (not) know'**
32. that you should succeed—connected with the adjective **'desirous'**

EXERCISE 40

1. that Jack built—qualifies the noun **'house'**
2. that climbs too high—qualifies the pronoun **'He'**
3. that knows no waking—qualifies the noun **'sleep'**
4. (that) the teacher gave us—qualifies the noun **'order'**
5. that are honest—qualifies the noun **'Servants'**
6. who die in a great cause—qualifies the pronoun **'They'**
7. who love us—qualifies the pronoun **'those'**
8. which is lost—qualifies the noun **'moment'**
9. which goes in and out with me—qualifies the noun **'shadow'**

10.   that blows nobody good—qualifies the noun 'wind'
11.   when the seeds of character are sown—qualifies the noun 'time'
12.   that sailed the wintry sea—qualifies the noun 'Hesperus'
13.   who have done the wrong—qualifies the pronoun 'They'
14.   who has made a name for himself—qualifies the noun 'son'
15.   who helps you in time of need—qualifies the noun 'friend'
16.   that glitters—qualifies the pronoun 'All'
17.   (that) I asked him—qualifies the noun 'question'
18.   who laughs last—qualifies the pronoun 'He'
19.   (that) we enjoy—qualifies the noun 'blessings'
20.   that are whole—qualifies the pronoun 'They'
21.   who are great boasters—qualifies the noun 'men'
22.   (that) you propose—qualifies the noun 'plan'
23.   that never finds the day—qualifies the noun 'night'
24.   that has no turning—qualifies the noun 'lane'
25.   (that) I asked for—qualifies the pronoun 'everything'
26.   that he laid his hands upon—qualifies the pronoun 'everything'
27.   that remind me of his father—qualifies the noun 'tricks'
28.   (that) you sent me—qualifies the noun 'message'
29.   which hung over the garden wall—qualifies the noun 'grapes'
30.   that held a prince—qualifies the noun 'bark'
31.   that is down—qualifies the pronoun 'He'
32.   as dreams are made of'—qualifies the noun 'stuff'
33.   that hath no music in his soul—qualifies the noun 'man'
34.   Which God has given to man alone beneath the heaven—qualifies the noun 'gift'
35.   Where our hero we buried—qualifies the noun 'grave'
36.   Who lives longest—qualifies the pronoun 'he' (understood)
37.   That is seated by the sea—qualifies the noun 'town'

EXERCISE 41

This is the book *I want*.
He is not a person *I would trust*.
The car *I hired* broke down after five miles.
This is the most interesting novel *I have ever read*.
The book *I was reading last night* was a detective novel.
The boy you *see at the door* is my nephew.
The pen *I lost* was not a good one.
The ladder *I was standing on* began to slip.
One of the people *I work with* has won the first prize in the lottery.
What is the name of the woman *you were speaking to*?

EXERCISE 42

I was not here on the day *he arrived*.
The time *he was born* was very auspicious.
This is the occasion *you should prove your worth*.
The reason *he came* was to borrow my bicycle.
Do you know the year *Pandit Nehru died*?
I don't know the time *the accident happened*.
This is the place *I lost my ring*.
Can you tell me the time *the meeting will begin*?
I can never forget the day *I first met* you.
The time *he will arrive is uncertain*.

EXERCISE 43

Wait here *till I come back*.
When we reached the station the train had departed.
She fell down *while she was getting off the bus*.
We shall go *as soon as you are ready*.
I shall see him *before I leave for England*.

EXERCISE 44

You may sit *where you like*.
I have put it back *where I found it*.
She shall have music *wherever she goes*.

EXERCISE 45

He is studying hard *so that he can get a first class*.
Bring it nearer *that I may see it better*
I didn't move *lest I should wake him up*

EXERCISE 46

I didn't buy it *because it was very expensive*
We must finish now, *since it is nearly bedtime*
Since you don't take advice, there is no point in asking for it.
As it is raining, you'd better stay indoors.
The boy was absent *because he was ill*.

EXERCISE 47

She will come *if you telephone her*.
Unless you work hard you cannot pass the examination.
If you heat ice it turns to water.

If I were you I wouldn't do that.
You can't get there in time *unless you take a taxi*.

═══ EXERCISE 48 ═══

It was so dark *that I could see nothing*.
He ran so quickly *that we couldn't catch him*.
His speech went on so long *that I fell asleep*.
So terrible was the storm that *many houses collapsed*.
It's such a good story *that I'll never forget it*.

═══ EXERCISE 49 ═══

I can't walk as fast *as you can*.
Life is as pleasant *as you make it*.
He is not so stupid *as he looks*.
She is much older *than she looks*.
You are not as clever *as she is*.

═══ EXERCISE 50 ═══

You should do *as I tell you*.
Leave it *as it is*.
As you sow, you will reap.
Write *as I suggest*.
You may finish it *how you like*.

═══ EXERCISE 51 ═══

Although it was raining, he went out without a raincoat.
Though he was wealthy, he was not happy·
Even if you don't like him, you can still be polite.
I'll buy one *whatever it costs*.
However often I tried, I could not find the answer.

═══ EXERCISE 52 ═══

1. as we forgive our enemies—Adverb Clause of Manner, modifying the verb 'forgive'
2. that we may reap—Adverb Clause of Purpose, modifying the verb **'sow'**
3. as I told him—Adverb Clause of Manner, modifying the verb **'did'**
4. if I tried—Adverb Clause of Condition, modifying the verb **'couldn't be'**
5. as we were setting out—Adverb Clause of Time, modifying the verb **'arrived'**

6. If this story were false—Adverb Clause of Condition, modifying the verb **'should do'**

7. since I had nothing to eat—Adverb Clause of Time, modifying the verb **'is'**

8. wherever I go—Adverb Clause of Place, modifying the verb **'make'**

9. as the Romans (do)—Adverb Clause of Manner, modifying the verb **'do'**

10. If I were you—Adverb Clause of Condition, modifying the verb **'would do'**

11. as his word (was)—Adverb Clause of Degree, modifying the adjective **'good'**

12. as yours (is)—Adverb Clause of Degree, modifying the adjective **'keen'**

13. where there was no earth—Adverb Clause of Place, modifying the verb **'fell'**

14. Since you say so—Adverb Clause of Reason, modifying the verb **'must believe'**

15. if you value your life—Adverb Clause of Condition, modifying the verb **'stand'**

16. that he may become rich—Adverb Clause of Purpose, modifying the verb **'labours'**

17. than he could afford—Adverb Clause of Degree, modifying the adverb **'more'**

18. that a child can understand it—Adverb Clause of Result, modifying the adjective **'simple'**

19. as though he did not hear—Adverb Clause of Manner, modifying the verb **'kept on'**

20. Boy as he was—Adverb Clause of Concession, modifying the verb **'was chosen'**

21. as a cowboy rides—Adverb Clause of Manner, modifying the verb **'rides'**

22. before I submit—Adverb Clause of Time, modifying the verb **'will die'**

23. as he was returning from school—Adverb Clause of Time, modifying the verb **'was caught'**

24. than he writes—Adverb Clause of Degree, modifying the verb **'speaks'**

25. while I was out—Adverb Clause of Time, modifying the verb **'came'**

26. After the vote was taken—Adverb Clause of Time, modifying the verb **'broke up'**

27. as if he had been a child—Adverb Clause of Manner, modifying the verb **'wept'**

28. as long as the Roman empire lasted—Adverb Clause of Time, modifying the verb **'was worshipped'**

29. as best he might—Adverb Clause of Manner, modifying the verb **'consoled'**

30. that I could not overtake him—Adverb Clause of Result, modifying the adverb **'fast'**

31. in as much as I have told him—Adverb Clause of Reason, modifying the verb ·knows·

32. that (he has) brains—Adverb Clause of Degree, modifying the Adjective ·more·

33. Since you desire it—Adverb Clause of Reason, modifying the verb 'will look'

34. lest any one should escape—Adverb Clause of Purpose, modifying the verb 'set'

35. although his success was not expected—Adverb Clause of Concession, modifying the verb ·succeeded'

36. than the moon (is)—Adverb Clause of Degree, modifying the adjective 'larger'

37. when the cannonading stopped all of a sudden—Adverb Clause of Time, modifying the verb ·was'

38. ere charity began—Adverb Clause of Time, modifying the verb 'gave'

39. wherever I went—Adverb Clause of Time, modifying the verb 'was'

40. as if the ground were slipping beneath his feet—Adverb Clause of Manner, modifying the verb 'felt'

41. as though they could do no wrong—Adverb Clause of Manner, modifying the verb 'act'

42. where angels fear to tread—Adverb Clause of Place, modifying the verb 'rush'

43. lest he should be seen—Adverb Clause of Purpose, modifying the verb 'dared not stir'

44. before it was fairly started—Adverb Clause of Time, modifying the verb 'was checked'

45. that he may eat—Adverb Clause of Purpose, modifying the verb 'lives'

46. as (it) had been expected—Adverb Clause of Manner, modifying the verb 'happened'

47. when he discovered the print of a foot on the sand—Adverb Clause of Time, modifying the verb 'was puzzled'

48. as a feast (is)—Adverb Clause of Time, modifying the adjective 'good .

49. as the clock struck five—Adverb Clause of Time, modifying the verb 'finished'

50. as you stand there—Adverb Clause of Degree, modifying the adjective 'sure'

51. since my playmates left—Adverb Clause of Reason, modifying the verb 'is'

52. Whilst I live—Adverb Clause of Time, modifying the verb 'shall want'

53. than it carried conviction with it—Adverb Clause of Degree, modifying the adverb 'sooner'

54. Notwithstanding that Dunne is being lionized—Adverb Clause of Concession, modifying the verb 'keeps'

55. till the signal was given—Adverb Clause of Time, modifying the infinitive 'to wait'

56. Rich as he is—Adverb Clause of Degree, modifying the verb 'would envy'

57. than secret love (is)—Adverb Clause of Degree, modifying the adjective 'better'

58. that you keep your eye on me like this—Adverb Clause of Reason, modifying the verb 'have turned'

59. when the expression of his face began to change—Adverb Clause of Time, modifying the verb 'had read'

60. as I intended him for the learned profession—Adverb Clause of Reason, modifying the verb 'was bred'

61. as enabled him to view with the first grandees of England—Adverb Clause of Extent, modifying the adjective 'such'

62. before I began to think seriously of matrimony—Adverb Clause of Time, modifying the verb 'had taken'

63. If you have tears—Adverb Clause of Condition, modifying the verb 'have'

64. as long as men are men—Adverb Clause of Time, modifying the verb 'will be'

EXERCISE 53

1. He talked so long *that he was tired*. (Adverb Clause of result, modifying 'so long')

2. I asked *where he was born*. (Noun Clause, object of 'asked')

3. He did *as he was told*. (Adverb Clause of manner, modifying 'did')

4. I don't believe *what you say*. (Noun Clause, subject of 'don't believe')

5. *Whosoever* is guilty will be punished. (Noun Clause, subject of 'will be punished)

6. He laughs best *who laughs last*. (Adjective Clause, qualifying 'he')

7. People like him *because he is generous*. (Adverb Clause of reason, modifying 'like')

8. I shall help you, *since you say so*. (Adverb Clause of reason, modifying 'shall help')

9. He was punished *as he deserved*. (Adverb Clause of manner, modifying 'was punished')

10. He mended his ways *before it was late*. (Adverb Clause of time modifying 'mended')

11. He rushed home a*s soon as he heard the news*. (Adverb Clause of time modifying 'rushed')

12. He drove so fast *that he soon overtook me*. (Adverb Clause of result, modifying 'so fast')

13. He found the umbrella *where he had left it*. (Adverb Clause of place, modifying 'found')

14. I asked him *how old he was*. (Noun Clause, object of 'asked)

15. *If you are diligent*, you will learn Hindi in a few weeks. (Adverb Clause of condition, modifying 'will learn')

16. I stopped *because I was tired*. (Adverb Clause of reason, modifying 'stopped')

17. We don't know *what has become of him*. (Noun Clause, object of 'don't know')

18. Let us find out *when the train will arrive*. (Noun Clause, object of 'find out')

19. Do you know *who did it*? (Noun Clause, object of 'do know')

20. Do *whatever you think right*. (Noun Clause, object of 'do')

21. I haven't seen him *since I returned from Lahore*. (Adverb Clause of time, modifying 'haven't seen')

22. I wonder *how this will end*. (Noun Clause, object of 'wonder')

23. Ask him *what he wants*. (Noun Clause, object of 'ask')

24. He ran as fast *as he could*. (Adverb Clause of degree, modifying 'as fast')

25. We couldn't get the information *as he was not there*. (Adverb Clause of reason, object of 'couldn't get')

26. I would accept the offer *if I were you*. (Adverb Clause of condition, object of 'would accept')

27. It rained *so hard that the streets were flooded*. (Adverb Clause of result, modifying 'so hard')

28. He did it *as I told him*. (Adverb Clause of manner, modifying 'did')

29. I will die *before I submit*. (Adverb Clause of time, modifying 'will die')

30. I am told *that he is a millionaire*. (Noun Clause, object of 'am told')

31. She is as intelligent *as she is beautiful*. (Adverb Clause of degree, modifying 'as intelligent')

32. Tell me *what you want*. (Noun Clause, object of 'tell')

33. He was in Mumbai *when his father died.* (Adverb Clause of time, modifying 'was')

34. I didn't go out *as it was raining*. (Adverb Clause of reason, modifying 'didn't go')

35. You may *do as you please.* (Adverb Clause of manner, modifying 'may do')

36. He is stronger *than you are*. (Adverb Clause of degree, modifying 'stronger')

37. *Although he is not rich*, he has contributed liberally to the Red Cross. (Adverb Clause of concession, modifying 'has contributed')

38. Success attends the person *who works hard*. (adjective Clause, qualifying 'person')

39. I expect *that we shall win*. (Noun Clause, object of 'expect')

40. I can't say *when I shall return.* (Noun Clause, object of 'can't say')

41. You would not have succeeded, *if I had not helped you*. (Adverb Clause

of condition, modifying 'would not have succeeded')

42. They were defeated *although they fought most valiantly*. (Adverb Clause of concession, modifying 'were defeated')

43. *When the cat is away,* the mice play. (Adverb Clause of time, modifying 'play')

44. Strike the iron *while it is hot.* (Adverb Clause of time, modifying 'strike')

45. God helps those *who help themselves*. (Adverb Clause, qualifying 'those')

46. Make hay *while the sun shines.* (Adverb Clause of time, modifying 'make')

47. Be cautious *till you are out of the wood*. (Adverb Clause of time, modifying 'be')

48. Uneasy lies the head *that wears a crown.* (Adjective Clause, qualifying 'head')

49. Those *who live in glass houses* should not throw stones. (Adjective Clause, qualifying 'those')

50. *Where ignorance is bliss* it is folly to be wise. (Adverb Clause of place, modifying 'is')

51. It is an ill wind *that blows nobody good*. (Adjective Clause, qualifying 'it')

52. *No sooner did he see me* than he ran away. (Adverb Clause of time, modifying 'ran')

53. We are such stuff *as dreams are made of*. (Adjective Clause, qualifying 'such stufff')

54. It is a long lane *that has no turning*. (Adjective Clause, qualifying 'It')

55. Fools rush in *where angels fear to tread*. (Adverb Clause of place, modifying 'rush')

56. We eat *that we may live*. (Adverb Clause of purpose, modifying 'eat')

EXERCISE 54

1. We don't know *where he was buried*. (Noun Clause, object of 'don't know')

Where he was buried is not known. (Noun Clause, subject of 'is not known')

It is not known *where he was buried*. (Noun Clause, put in apposition to 'It')

This is the place *where he was buried*. (Adjective Clause, qualifying 'place')

A tomb-stone was set up *where he was buried*. (Adverb Clause of place, modifying 'was set up')

2. Can you tell me, *when the train will arrive*? (Noun Clause, object of 'can tell')

When the train will arrive is uncertain. (Noun Clause, subject of 'is')

It is uncertain *when the train will arrive*. (Noun Clause, put in apposition to 'It')

Would you please tell me the time *when the train will arrive*? (Adjective Clause, qualifying 'time')

3. He couldn't say *where he had left it*. (Noun Clause, object of 'couldn't say')

Where he had left it was not known. (Noun Clause, subject of 'was not known')

It was not known *where he had left it*. (Noun Clause, put in apposition to 'It')

The pen was found *where he had left it*. (Adverb Clause of place, modifying 'was found')

He didn't remember the place *where he had left it*. (Adjective Clause, qualifying 'place')

4. Do you know *who did it*? (Noun Clause, object of 'do know')

Who did it is a mystery. (Noun Clause, subject of 'is')

It is a mystery *who did it*. (Noun Clause, put in apposition to 'It')

I saw the man *who did it*. (Noun Clause, qualifying 'man')

5. Ask him *why he did it*. (Noun Clause, object of 'ask')

Why he did it cannot be explained. (Noun Clause, subject of 'cannot be explained')

It is not known *why he did it*. (Noun Clause, put in apposition to 'It')

The reason *why he did it* still remains a mystery. (Noun Clause, put in apposition to 'reason')

This is *why he did it*. (Noun Clause, complement of 'is')

6. I believed *that he might succeed in life*. (Noun Clause, object of 'believed')

That he might succeed in life was my belief. (Noun Clause, subject of 'was')

My belief was *that he might succeed in life*. (Noun Clause, complement of 'was')

It was my belief *that he might succeed in life*. (Noun Clause, put in apposition to 'It')

He worked hard *that he might succeed in life*. (Adverb Clause of purpose, modifying 'worked')

7. I asked him *whom he had met*. (Noun Clause, object of 'asked')

Whom he had met was not known. (Noun Clause, subject of 'was not known')

It was not clear *whom he had met*. (Noun Clause, put in apposition to 'It')

The man *whom he had met* cheated him. (Adjective Clause, qualifying 'man')

The man *whom he had met* cheated him. (Adjective Clause, qualifying 'man')

8. Can you say *when the monsoon failed*? (Noun Clause, object of 'can say')

   When the monsoon failed is not exactly known. (Noun Clause, subject of 'is not known')

   It is not exactly known *when the monsoon failed*. (Noun Clause, put in apposition to 'It')

   Do you remember the year *when the monsoon failed*? (Adjective Clause, qualifying 'year')

   When the monsoon failed, our country suffered from famine. (Adverb Clause of time, modifying 'suffered')

EXERCISE 55

1. if 2. if 3. who/that 4. that 5. than 6. who/that 7. that/which 8. as 9. that/ who, till 10. that/which 11. Though 12. that 13. that/who 14. though/although 15. If 16. When 17. than 18. If 19. Though...yet 20. how 21. If 22. When 23. since 24. which/that 25. as 26. when 27. When/After, who 28. who/that 29. when 30. where 31. When 32. till 33. when 34. who/that 35. till/until, who 36. who/that 37. that 38. who/that, where 39. that 40. Since 41. though / although 42. while 43. When, who, that 44. that, till 45. Where/who, how 46. that, when 47. Though/Although, and 48. why, that 49. that, when

EXERCISE 56

1. (a) I determined to send him to town (Principal Clause)
   (b) As my eldest son was bred a scholar [Adverb Clause of reason, modifying 'determined' in (a)]
   (c) where the abilities might contribute......his own [Adjective Clause, qualifying 'town' in (a)]
2. (a) Clive had been only a few months in the army (Principal Clause)
   (b) when intelligence arrived [Adverb Clause of time, modifying 'had been' in (a)]
   (c) that peace had been.......and France [Noun Clause, put in apposition to 'intelligence' in (b)]
3. (a) I had a partial father (Principal Clause)
   (b) who gave me a better education [Adjective Clause, qualifying 'father' in (a)]
   (c) than his broken fortune would have allowed [Adverb Clause of degree, modifying 'better' in (b)]
4. (a) He told us (Principal Clause)
   (b) that he had read Milton in a prose translation [Noun Clause, object of 'told' in (a)]
   (c) when he was fourteen [Adverb Clause of time, modifying 'had read' in (b)]

5. (a) he will always find his happiness incomplete (Principal Clause)
   (b) with whatever luxuries a bachelor may be surrounded [Adverb Clause of concession, modifying 'will find' in (a)]
   (c) unless he has a wife and children [Adverb Clause of condition, modifying 'will find' in (a)]

6. (a) Among many reasons, one of the first is (Principal Clause)
   (b) which make me glad to have been born in England [Adjective Clause, qualifying 'reasons' in (a)]
   (c) that I read Shakespeare in my mother tongue [Noun Clause, complement of 'is' in (a)]

7. (a) He professed to have learned his poetry from Dryden (Principal Clause)
   (b) whom he praised through his whole life with unvaried liberality [Adjective Clause, qualifying 'Dryden' in (a)]
   (c) whenever an opportunity was presented [(Adverb Clause of time, modifying 'praised' in (b)]

8. (a) We hardly realize (Principal Clause)
   (b) who are fortunate to live in this enlightened century [Adjective Clause, qualifying 'we' in (a)]
   (c) how our ancestors suffered....beings [Noun Clause, object of 'realize' in (a)]

9. (a) We cannot justly interpret the religion of any people (Principal Clause)
   (b) unless we are prepared to admit [Adverb Clause of condition, modifying 'cannot interpret' in (a)]
   (c) that we ourselves are liable....faith [Noun Clause, object of 'to admit' in (b)]

10. (a) Milton said (Principal Clause)
    (b) that he did not educate his daughters in the languages [Noun Clause, object of 'said' in (a)]
    (c) because one tongue was enough for a woman [Adverb Clause of reason, modifying 'did (not) educate' in (b)]

11. (a) The man is a fool (Principal Clause)
    (b) who does not see [Adjective Clause, qualifying 'man' in (a)]
    (c) that the good of every living creature is his good [Noun Clause, object of 'does (not) see' in (b)]

12. (a) Nothing can describe the confusion of thought (Principal clasuse)
    (b) which I felt [Adjective Clause, qualifying 'man' in (a)]
    (c) when I sank into the water [Adverb Clause of time, modifying 'felt' in (b)]

13. (a) We had in this village, some twenty years ago, a boy (Principal Clause)
    (b) whom I well remember [Adjective Clause, qualifying 'boy' in (a)]

(c) who from his childhood showed.....for bees [Adjective Clause, qualifying 'boy' in (a)]

14. (a) Considering we are not to be surprised (Principal Clause).

(b) that the world is so intricate [Noun Clause, object of 'considering' in (a)]

(c) that science has progressed slowly. [Adverb Clause of result, modifying 'so intricate' in (b)]

15. (a) You take my house (Principal Clause)

(b) when you do take the prop [Adverb Clause of time, modifying 'take' in (b)]

(c) that both sustain my house [Adjective Clause, qualifying 'prop' in (b)]

16. (a) I heard a thousand blended notes (Principal Clause)

(b) while in a grove I sat reclined in that sweet mood [Adverb Clause of time, modifying 'heard' in (b)]

(c) when pleasant thoughts bring sad thoughts to the mind [Adverb Clause of time, modifying 'sat' in (b)]

17. (a) we cannot agree with Dr. Johnson (Principal Clause)

(b) Much as we like Shakespeare's (Adverb Clause of concession, modifying 'cannot agree')

(c) that they are better (Noun Clause, object of 'cannot agree')

(d) than his tragedies (are) [Adverb Clause, of degree, modifying 'better' in (c)]

18. (a) Those will find (Principal Clause)

(b) who look into practical life [Adjective Clause, qualifying 'those' in (a)]

(c) that fortune is usually on the side of the industrious [Noun Clause, object of 'will find' in (a)]

(d) as the winds and waves are on the side of the best navigators [Adverb Clause of comparison, modifying 'is' in (c)]

19. (a) He hardly knows (Principal Clause)

(b) who sits from day to day, heedless of its loudest lay [Adjective Clause, qualifying 'he' in (a)]

(c) that it has sung (Noun Clause, object of 'knows')

20. (a) History says (principal Clause)

(b) that Socrates continued to talk to the friends [Noun Clause, object of 'says' in (a)]

(c) when he was given the cup of hemlock [Adverb Clause of time, modifying 'continued' in (a)]

(d) who were standing around him [Adjective Clause, qualifying 'friends' in (b)]

21. (a) I have no sympathy with the poor man (Principal Clause)
    (b) (whom) I knew [Adjective Clause, qualifying 'man' in (a)]
    (c) who told me [Adjective Clause, qualifying 'man' in (a)]
    (d) (that) he dared not look at his razor [Noun Clause, object of 'told' in (c)]
    (e) when suicides abounded [Adverb Clause of time, modifying 'told' in (c)]

EXERCISE 57

1. (a) I am satisfied with things [Principal Clause]
   (b) as they are [Adverb Clause of manner or state, modifying 'am satisfied' in (a)]
   (c) and it will be my pride and pleasure to hand down this country to my children [Principal Clause, co-ordinate with (a)]
   (d) as I received it from those [Adverb Clause of state or manner, modifying 'to hand down' in (c)]
   (e) Who preceded me [Adjective Clause, qualifying 'there' in (d)]
2. (a) Some politicians of our time lay....proposition [Principal Clause]
   (b) that no people ought to be free [Noun Clause , put in apposition to 'it' in (a)]
   (c) till they are fit to use their freedom [Adverb Clause of time, object of 'ought to be']
3. (a) He never speaks of himself except [Principal Clause]
   (b) (that he speaks) [Noun Clause, object of 'except' in (a)]
   (c) when (he is) compelled [Adverb Clause of time, modifying 'speaks' in (b)]
   (d) (he) never defends himself by a mere retort [Principal Clause, coordinate with (a)]
   (e) he has no ears for slander or gossip [Principal Clause, co-ordinate with (a) and (d)]
   (f) (he) is scrupulous in imputing motives to those [Principal Clause, co-ordinate with (a), (d), and (e)]
   (g) who interfere with him [Adjective Clause, qualifying 'those' in (f)]
   (h) and (he) interprets everything for the best [Principal Clause, coordinate with (a), (d), (e) and (f)]
4. (a) Subhash Chandra Bose died [Principal Clause]
   (b) before his aim was achieved [Adverb Clause of time, object of 'died' in (a)]
   (c) and yet he will always....great hero [Principal Clause, coordinate with (a)]
   (d) who fought [Adjective Clause, qualifying 'hero' in (c)]

(e) and sacrificed his life....country [Adjective Clause, coordinate with (d) and qualifying 'hero']

5. (a) The notice had been kind [Principal Clause]

(b) which you have been pleased to take of my labours [Adjective Clause, qualifying 'notice' in (a)]

(c) had it been early [Adverb Clause of condition, modifying 'had been' in (a)]

(d) but it has been delayed [Principal Clause, co-ordinate with (a)]

(e) till I am indifferent [Adverb Clause of time, modifying 'has been delayed' in (d)]

(f) and (till) I cannot enjoy it [Adverb Clause of time co-ordinate with (e) and modifying 'has been delayed' in (d)]

6. (a) I hope [Principal Clause]

(b) (that) it is very cynical asperity not to confess obligations, or to be unwilling [Noun Clause, object of 'hope' in (a)]

(c) where no benefit has been received [Adverb Clause of place, modifying 'to confess' in (b)]

(d) that the public should consider me as owing that to a patron [Noun Clause, adjunct to 'unwilling' in (b)]

(e) which Providence has enabled me to do for myself [Adjective Clause, qualifying 'that' in (d)]

7. (a) I found [Principal Clause]

(b) while I was doing this [Adverb Clause of time, modifying 'found' in (a)]

(c) (that) the ride began to flow [Noun Clause, object of 'found' in (a)]

(d) though (it was) very calm [Adverb Clause of concession, modifying 'began' in (c)]

(e) and I had the mortification to see my coat, shirt and waistcoat swim away [Principal Clause, co-ordinate with (a)]

(f) which I had left on shore upon the sand [Adjective Clause, qualifying 'coat, shirt and waistcoat' in (e)

8. (a) with reluctance he accepted the invitations of his kindly and faithful Persian friend [Principal Clause]

(b) who scolded him for refusing meat [Adjective Clause, qualifying 'friend' in (a)]

(c) but he replied [Principal Clause, co-ordinate with (a)]

(d) that too much eating led man to commit many sins [Noun Clause, object of 'replied' in (c)]

9. (a) Macaulay had wealth and fame, rank and power [Principal Clause]

(b) and yet he tells us in his biography [Principal Clause, co-ordinate with (a)]

   (c) that he owed the happiest hours of his life to books [Noun Clause, object of 'tells' in (b)]

10. (a) A literary education is simply one of different kinds of education [Principal Clause]

   (b) and it is not wise [Prinicpal Clause, co-ordinate with (a)]

   (c) that more than a small percentage of the people of any country should have an exclusively literary education [Noun Clause, put in apposition to 'it' in (b)]

11. (a) The way into my parlour is up a winding stair [Principal Clause]

   (b) and I have many curious things to show [Principal Clause, co-ordinate with (a)]

   (c) when you are there [Adverb Clause of time, modifying 'to show' in (b)]

12. (a) They love to see the flaming forge and hear the bellows roar and catch the burning sparks [Principal Clause]

   (b) that fly like chaff from a threshing floor [Adjective Clause, qualifying 'sparks' in (a)]

13. (a) The friends came back every one [Principal Clause]

   (b) who had left [Adjective Clause, qualifying 'friends' in (a)]

   (c) And darkest advisers looked bright [Principal Clause, co-ordinate with (a)]

   (d) as the sun (does) [Adverb Clause of comparison, modifying 'bright' in (c)]

14. (a) She lived unknown [Principal Clause]

   (b) and few could know [Principal Clause, co-ordinate with (a)]

   (c) when Lucy ceased to be [Noun Clause, object of 'could know' in (b)]

15. (a) Three wives sat up in the lighthouse tower [Principal Clause]

   (b) And they trimmed the lamps [Principal Clause, co-ordinate with (a)]

   (c) as the sun went down [Adverbial Clause of time, modifying 'trimmed' in (b)]

16. (a) His hair was yellow [Principal Clause]

   (b) as hay (is) [Adverb Clause of comparison, modifying 'yellow' in (a)]

   (c) But threads of a silvery grey gleamed in his tawny beard [Principal Clause, co-ordinate with (a)]

EXERCISE 58

1. (a) He espied an old man stooping and leaning on his staff, weary with age and travel, coming towards him [Principal Clause]

- **(b)** when Abraham sat at his tent door, according to his custom, waiting to entertain strangers [Adverb Clause of time, modifying 'espied' in (a)]
- **(c)** who was a hundred years of age [Adjective Clause of time, qualifying 'man' in (a)]

2. **(a)** God called to Abraham [Principal cause]
   - **(b)** and (he) asked him [Principal Clause, co-ordinate with (a)]
   - **(c)** when the old man was gone [Adverb Clause of time, modifying 'called' in (a) and 'asked' in (b)]
   - **(d)** where the stranger was [Noun Clause, object of 'asked' in (b)]

3. **(a)** He replied [Principal Clause]
   - **(b)** (that) I thrust him away [Noun Clause, object of 'replied' in (a)]
   - **(c)** because he did not worship Thee (Adverb Clause of reason, modifying 'thrust']

4. **(a)** (you) enjoy the good things [Principal Clause]
   - **(b)** while you are upon earth [Adverb Clause of time, modifying 'enjoy' in (a)]
   - **(c)** that are here [Adjective Clause, qualifying 'things' in (a)]
   - **(d)** To that end they were given [Parenthetical Clause]
   - **(e)** and (you) be not melancholy [Principal Clause, co-ordinate with (a) and (e)]
   - **(f)** and (you do not) wish yourself in heaven [Principal Clause, co-ordinate with (a) and (e)]

5. **(a)** There is no saying [Principal Clause]
   - **(b)** (that) shocks me so much [Adjective Clause, qualifying 'saying' in (a)]
   - **(c)** as that (shocks) [Adverb Clause of comparison, modifying 'much' in (b)]
   - **(d)** which I hear very often [Adjective Clause, qualifying 'that' in (c)]
   - **(e)** that a man does not know how to pass his time [Noun Clause, put in apposition to 'that' in (e)]

6. **(a)** You must observe, my friend [Principal Clause]
   - **(b)** that it is the custom of this country for the company to sit as mute and as motionless [Noun Clause, object of 'must observe' in (a)]
   - **(c)** as statues (do) [Adverb Clause of comparison, modifying 'mute' and 'motionless' in (b)]
   - **(d)** when a lady or gentleman happens to sing [Adverb Clause of time, modifying 'to sit' as in (a)]

7. **(a)** Mr. Burchell had scarce taken leave [Principal Clause]
   - **(b)** and Sophia (had scarce) consented to dance with the Chaplain [Principal Clause, co-ordinate with (a)]

(c) when my little ones came running out to tell us [Adverb Clause of time, modifying 'had taken' in (a) and (had) consented' in (b)]

(d) that the Squire had come with a crowd of company [Noun Clause, object of 'to tell' in (c)]

8. (a) I hope [Principal Clause]

(b) (that) it will give comfort to great numbers [Noun Clause, object of 'hope' in (a)]

(c) who are passing through the world in obscurity [Adjective Clause, qualifying 'numbers' in (b)]

(d) when I inform them [Adverb Clause of time, modifying 'will give' in (b)]

(e) How easily distinction may be obtained [Noun Clause, object of 'inform' in (b)]

9. (a) All have done good work [Principal Clause]

(b) who have meant good work with their whole hearts [Adjective Clause, qualifying 'all' in (a)]

(c) although they may die [Adverb Clause of concession, modifying 'have done' in (a)]

(d) before they have the time to sign it [Adverb Clause of time, modifying 'may die' in (c)]

10. (a) We are told [Principal Clause]

(b) that he stole from his play-fellows to a vault in St. Jame's fields for purpose of investigating the cause of a singular echo [Noun Clause, object of 'are told' in (a)]

(c) while (he was) still a mere child [Adverb Clause of time, modifying 'stole' in (b)]

(d) which he had observed there [Adjective Clause, qualifying 'echo' in (b)]

11. (a) the slave, hearing the shrieks of the dying person, ran to see [Principal Clause]

(b) who was at his work not far from the place [Adjective Clause, qualifying 'slave' in (a)]

(c) where this astonishing piece of cruelty was committed [Adjective Clause, qualifying 'place' in (b)]

(d) what was the occasion of them (Noun Clause, object of 'to see' in (a)]

12. (a) Every insignificant author fancies it of importance to the world to know [Principal Clause]

(b) that he wrote his book in the country [Noun Clause, object of 'to know' in (a)]

(c) that he did it to pass away some of his idle hours [Noun Clause, co-ordinate with (b) and object of 'to know' in (a)]

(d) that it was published at the importunity of friends [Noun Clause, co-ordinate with (a) and (c) and object of 'to know' in (a)]

(e) that his natural temper, studies or conversation directed him to the choice of his subject [Noun Clause, co-ordinate with (a), (b), (c) and (d) and object of 'to know' in (a)]

13. (a) I consider a human soul without education like marble in a quarry [Principal Clause]

(b) which shows none of its inherent beauties [Adjective Clause, qualifying 'marble' in (a)]

(c) until the skill of the polisher fetches out the colours [Adverb Clause of time, modifying 'shows' in (b)]

(d) (until it) makes the surface shine [Adverb Clause of time, co-ordinate with (c) and modifying 'shows' in (b)]

(e) (until it) discovers every ornamental cloud, spot and view [Adverb Clause of time, co-ordinate with (c) and (d) and modifying 'shows' in (b)]

(f) that run through the body of it [Adjective Clause, qualifying 'cloud', 'spot' and 'view' in (e)]

14. (a) They sent a message to the oracle of Jupiter Ammon to ask the reason [Principal Clause]

(b) when the Athenians in the war with the Lacedaemonians received many defeats both by sea and land [Adverb Clause of time, modifying 'sent' in (a)]

(c) why they should be less successful [Noun Clause, put in apposition to 'reason' in (a)]

(d) who erected so many temples to the gods [Adjective Clause, qualifying 'they' in (c)]

(e) (and who) adorned them with such costly offerings [Adjective Clause, coordinate with (d) and qualifying 'they' in (c)]

(f) than the Lacedaemonians (were) [Adverb Clause of comparison, modifying 'less successful' in (c)]

(g) who fell so short of them in all these particulars [Adjective Clause, qualifying 'Lacedaemonians' in (f)]

15. (a) He feels not the wants nor plagues [Principal Clause]

(b) that holds fast the golden mean [Adjective Clause qualifying 'he' in (a)]

(c) and (that) lives contentedly between the little and the great [Adjective Clause, co-ordinate with (b), qualifying 'he' in (a)]

(d) that pinch the poor [Adjective Clause, qualifying 'wants' in (a)]

(e) that haunt the rich man's door, embittering his state [Adjective Clause, qualifying 'plagues' in (a)]

EXERCISE 59

1.   It is never so late that one cannot mend.
2.   He is so proud that he cannot beg.
3.   My heart is so full that I cannot express my feelings.
4.   He was so late that he could not hear the first speech.
5.   He is so ignorant that he cannot be a postman.
6.   The boy was so old that he could not be a postman.
7.   This tree is so high that I cannot climb it.
8.   He speaks so fast that he cannot be understood.
9.   He is so stupid that he is not suitable for such a difficult post.
10. She was sobbing so deeply that she could not make any answer.
11. This fact is so evident that it does not require proof.
12. The work is so much that no man can do it single-handed.
13. That shirt is so small that it does not suit me.
14. The bag was so heavy that I could not carry it.

EXERCISE 60

1.   His (Abdul's) brother is not stronger than Abdul.   (Comparative)
2.   Akbar was greater than most other kings.   (Comparative)
3.   Karim is not more industrious than some other boys.   (Comparative)
     Karim is not the most industrious boy.   (Superlative)
4.   Mysore is not so cool as Bangalore.   (Positive)
5.   Rama is better than any other bowler in the eleven.   (Comparative)
     Rama is the best bowler in the eleven.   (Superlative)
6.   Chennai is bigger than most other cities in India.   (Comparative)
     Chennai is one of the biggest cities in India.   (Superlative)
7.   *The Arabian Nights* is more popular than any other storybook.

                                                               (Comparative)

     The Arabian Nights is the most popular storybook.   (Superlative)
8.   Your pony is not so well trained as this.   (Positive)
9.   No other church in Mumbai is so big as this.   (Positive)
     This church is bigger than any other church in Mumbai.(Comparative)
10. No other morning paper has as big a circulation as this newspaper.

                                                                   (Positive)

     This newspaper has the biggest circulation of all the morning
     papers.   (Superlative)
11. No other woman was so beautiful as Helen of Troy.   (Positive)
     Helen was the most beautiful woman.   (Superlative)

12. Birds do not fly as fast as airplane.   (Positive)
13. Very few Indian cities are as big as Hyderabad.   (Positive)
    Hyderabad is bigger than most other Indian cities.   (Comparative)
14. Meat is not more nutritious than some beans.   (Comparative)
15. Very few Indian kings were as great as Samudra Gupta.   (Positive)
    Samudra Gupta was greater than most other Indian kings.(Comparative)
16. No other island in the world is so large as Australia.   (Positive)
    Australia is larger than any other island in the world.   (Comparative)
17. India is larger than any other democracy in the world.   (Comparative)
    No other democracy in the world is as large as India.   (Positive)
18. This is larger than most other districts in India.   (Comparative)
    Very few districts in India are as large as this.   (Positive)
19. It is not so good to beg as to starve.   (Positive)
20. He does not love any of his sons better than the others.   (Comparative)

EXERCISE 61

1. This novel was written by Premchand.
2. The brave are admired (by us).
3. The baby was bought a ball. (or : A ball was bought for the baby.)
4. I am known to them.
5. I was invited to his house yesterday.
6. Bathing is enjoyed by them.
7. The door was opened by them.
8. The book was read by me long ago.
9. It was expected by Pakistan that they would win the match.
10. He was appointed monitor.
11. By whom were you taught such tricks as these?
12. Caesar was accused of ambition by Brutus.
13. The cliff is being climbed by the boy.
14. I was taught by him to read Persian.
15. Better behaviour is expected from a college student.
16. A video of 'The Titanic' was shown.
17. What cannot be cured must be endured.
18. The troops were reviewed by the General in the maidan.
19. We were shown some ancient coins by the curator of the museum.
    (or : Some ancient coins were shown us by the curator of the museum.)
20. The old house has been pulled down.
21. Passengers are forbidden to cross the railway line.
22. His wife was made to do the work.
23. Beasts are taught by Nature to know their friends.
24. Wealth is desired by all and acquired by some.

25. Four million African slaves were emancipated by Lincoln.
26. Good news is expected.
27. It is proposed to build a dam for irrigation purposes.
28. He was offered a chair. (or : A chair was offered him.)
29. Quebec was surrendered by the French to the English in 1759.
30. I was shown the greatest respect.
31. Alas! his voice will be heard no more.
32. Will those happy days be ever forgotten?
33. Is my meaning understood?
34. His words, must be listened to.

EXERCISE 62

1. It was hoped by Macbeth that he would succeed Duncan.
2. Who were you taught Urdu by? (Formal : By whom were your taught Urdu?)
3. He was found guilty of murder.
4. Orders that he should be imprisoned were immediately given by the King.
5. The light has been put out.
6. His warnings were laughed at and all his proposals (were) objected to.
7. He was regarded as an impostor and called a villain by the Swiss.
8. The money has been kept in the safe.
9. It was pretended by him that he was a baron.
10. He was accused of various offences by his subordinates.
11. He was seen opening the box.
12. The police were ordered to pursue the thief.
13. Grapes cannot be gathered from thistles.
14. A happy millionaire is never heard of.
15. It will be learnt with astonishment that war is imminent.
16. Was that name never heard?
17. We are told how the castle received its name.
18. Let not the weak be insulted.
19. Why were you defrauded of your earnings?

EXERCISE 63

1. The clerk wrote the letter.
2. Without effort one can gain nothing.
3. Kalidas wrote "Shakuntala."
4. His singular appearance struck me.
5. My brother saw him.
6. They chose him leader.

7. Bees make honey.
8. A cruel boy killed the bird.
9. Watt invented the steam-engine.
10. The cat killed the mouse.
11. The teacher praised the boy.
12. The Prince of Wales opened the Exhibition.
13. Who broke this jug?
14. They/He offered me a chair.
15. Everyone will blame us.
16. The sight will gladden him.
17. Alexander Graham Bell invented telephone.
18. Somebody has stolen my watch.
19. A cat may look at the king.
20. They have cut the telephone wires.
21. They pronounced harsh sentences on the offenders.
22. We will discuss this question at the meeting tomorrow.
23. Why should you suspect me?
24. Those who live in glass houses should not throw stones.
25. He will be greatly surprised if they choose him.
26. The crew set the ship on fire and abandoned it.
27. The police arrested him on a charge of theft, but for lack of evidence released him.

EXERCISE 64

1. A griffin was not so rapacious as he.
2. A griffin was not more rapacious than he.
3. No other Great Moghul was so great as Akbar.
4. Aurangzeb was not so great as he.
5. The rose by any other name would not smell less sweet.
6. No sooner did he come than they made objections.
7. I own no wealth other than these fishing nets.
8. I am never without love for my country.
9. No other mountain in the world is so high as Everest.
10. He is not always wise.
11. He did not notice me when he came in.
12. Nobody will deny that he did his best.
13. None but a millionaire can afford such extravagance.
14. There is no man who does not make mistake sometimes.
15. I do not care what he says about me.
16. No sooner did he see me than he came up and spoke to me.
17. He must not have failed to see the Taj Mahal when he went to Agra.

EXERCISE 65

1. Everybody was present.
2. He lived only a few years in India.
3. Everyone would admit that she was pretty.
4. God will remember the cry of the humble.
5. I am very tired.
6. Everyone present cheered.
7. Whenever I laid a plan in my life, I carried it out.
8. Only a few men would be cruel and unjust to a cripple.
9. He did as well as any man could have done.
10. The two brothers are alike.
11. He has promised to abstain from wine in future.
12. We found the road rather bad.
13. Where there is smoke there is fire.
14. It is likely that he has seen the home for the last time.

EXERCISE 66

1. No one can touch pitch without being defiled.
2. No man by taking thought can add a cubit of his stature.
3. It does not matter even if the field is lost.
4. That is not the way a gentleman should behave.
5. Everyone knows the owl.
6. I shall never forget those happy days.
7. No one is so wicked as to amuse himself with the infirmities of extreme old age.
8. You should not waste time in this fruitless occupation.
9. This is not the kind of dress to wear in school.
10. You cannot gather grapes from thorns or figs from thistles.

EXERCISE 67

1. Who can be expected to submit for ever to injustice?
2. Is there anything better than a busy life?
3. Where in the world will you find a fairer building than the Taj Mahal?
4. What is the use of offering bread to a man who is dying of thirst?
5. What could we have done without your help?
6. Was that an example to be followed?

EXERCISE 68

1. I would give anything to see you happy.
2. There was a wonderful (or : horrible sight).

3. Man is a wonderful piece of work.
4. Great things (or : wonderful things) might be done, if men were wise.
5. An elephant is a very wonderful creature.
6. He manages his sword very awkwardly.
7. I wish we two were infants playing.
8. I wish I had the wings of a dove.
9. He has a very large nose.
10. I wish I had a good horse.
11. I wish I were safe at home.
12. There was a great fall, my countrymen.
13. It was a very delicious meal.
14. A quiet life affords very sweet delight.
15. The camel is very well fitted for the work he has to do.
16. You are very cold.
17. This is a very beautiful scene.
18. These mangoes have a very delicious flavour.
19. It is shameful of you to use a poor cripple so.
20. I wish I knew more people.
21. You have grown very much.
22. I wish I had come one hour sooner.

EXERCISE 69

1. What a horrible night it is!
2. How base of him to desert you in your time of need!
3. How hard to believe that he did such a deed!
4. Had I met you ten years ago!
5. How stupid of me to forget your name!
6. What an unhappy life he leads!

EXERCISE 70

(a) 1. He rejected all that we *proposed*.
    2. Steel is *strengthened* by the addition of nickel.
    3. He *agreed* to supply me with firewood.
    4. What he *purposes* is not clear from his letter.
    5. You *cannot be admitted* without a ticket.
    6. He *does not intend* to leave the city
    7. I *am disinclined* to *work* today.
    8. He *succeeded* in all that he *undertook*.
    9. These mangoes *smell* sweet but *taste* sour.

(b) 1. The defenders *succeeded* in repelling every attack on the city.
    2. This scene *surpasses* all others in beauty.
    3. It is *admitted* that he is the greatest general of the century.
    4. They *rejoiced* most at the good news.

(c) 1. Though the ant is small it has as much *intelligence* as the elephant.
    2. He expressed *regret* for his hasty *act* (or : *action*)
    3. He was so full of *activity* in his old age that he won everybody's admiration.
    4. Before I pay you your *dues*, you must affix your *signature* to this receipt.
    5. The best way to maintain *health* is to observe *temperance* in all things.

(d) 1. It is quite probable that the day will be fine.
    2. The rats were greatly troublesome to us.
    3. He was dismissed for being *negligent* rather than for being incompetent.
    4. It was an *admitted* fact that he was clever, but it was *evident* that he lacked industry.
    5. The merchant was greatly *successful* in all his dealings, and it was *natural* that he was esteemed by his fellow citizens.

(e) 1. He was *poorly* and *meanly* dressed.
    2. He broke the rules without any intention of doing so, but it does not follow that he was *wrongly* punished.
    3. He was *evidently* mistaken but *obviously* sincere.
    4. By *carefully* analysing these substances you will see that they are *essentially* different.

EXERCISE 71

1. In his tower the poet sat and gazed on the sea.
2. The project completely failed and everyone was surprised.
3. We saw the rain coming on and took shelter under a tree.
4. He not only educated his nephew but also set him up in business.
5. The fog was very dense and so the steamer sailed at less than half speed.
6. Raleigh took off his cloak politely and placed it in the muddy street.
7. He was occupied with important matters and therefore had no leisure to see us.
8. He is popular, yet he cannot be called a great writer.
9. He rushed against Horatius and smote with all his might.
10. He was very learned, he was far from being a pedant.
11. Little Jack Horner sat in a corner and ate his Christmas pie.
12. He must resign, or he will be publicly dismissed.

13. There is drought and so the crop is short.
14. The sun set, and yet the men had not completed their work.
15. He made several efforts but failed.
16. He had pleasant manners and therefore gained many friends.
17. Not only did he give them pecuniary assistance, he also gave them much valuable advice.
18. The referee whistled and the game was stopped.
19. He was negligent and therefore the company suffered heavy losses.
20. He ran at top speed and got out of breath.
21. He possessed all the advantages of education and wealth and yet he never made a name.
22. The magician took pity on the mouse and turned it into a cat.
23. He was dissatisfied and so resigned his position.
24. He threw off his coat and plunged into the sea.

EXERCISE 72

1. The boys heard their father's footsteps and ran away.
2. He put forth a great effort and lifted the box.
3. The man was very hungry and so ate too much.
4. He was very strong, yet he was overcome.
5. His family did not like him to leave school, but he did. (or : He left school, and this was against the wishes of his family.)
6. He was virtuous and was therefore universally respected.
7. His friend has helped him, and so he is prospering.
8. He is a cripple and therefore cannot ride a horse.
9. The rain washed away the embankment and therefore the train was wrecked,
10. He found himself in difficulty and went to his teacher for help.
11. My friend is now in Mumbai and I shall go there to meet him.
12. Let such a thing happen and then I should take long leave.
13. They are forbidden to enter the sacred place and disobedience is punished with death.
14. You must apply early, or you cannot be certain of getting a place.
15. He has failed repeatedly, yet he intends to try again.
16. I have given him my advice, yet he has done this foolish thing..
17. He has great ability and therefore he has been able to win a high position.
18. He has become very poor, but it is not through any fault of his own.
19. He used very inaccurate language, for he knew no better.
20. His sword broke and he was left defenceless.
21. His health was bad and so he was rejected.
22. He is proud and boastful and therefore I do not like him.

23.   He wanted to avoid punishment and so he ran away.
24.   He was ignorant and therefore followed the wrong course.
25.   He has made no provision for old age and so he is poor.
26.   He had a desire for revenge and so he agreed to this.
27.   A tyre burst on the way and this added to their troubles.

EXERCISE 73

1.   Being poor, they often suffered great hardship.
2.   Having overslept himself, he missed the train.
3.   Slaying his brother, the prince became king in his place.
4.   This coat is too big to be mine.
5.   This general, having fought bravely, the king made him Com mander-in-Chief.
6.   Pushing his head into the tent, the camel asked to be allowed to warm his nose.
7.   Having never been at school as a boy, he had no opportunity of learning to read or write.
8.   In the event of its occurring again, you will be punished.
9.   Being unwilling to disappoint his friend, he granted the request.
10.   With all their precautions, they ran aground.
11.   In spite of his being rich, he is not contented.
12.   Make haste so as not to be late.
13.   In spite of the steamer going down, the crew were saved.
14.   The piper advancing, the children followed.
15.   The horse rearing, the rider was thrown.
16.   Walk quickly so as to overtake him.
17.   In spite of my calling him, he gave me no answer.
18.   In the event of some passing ship having not saved him, he must have been drowned.
19.   Being a conscientious man, he must have done his duty.
20.   In spite of his having tried hard, he did not succeed.
21.   In spite of his repeated attempts, he did not succeed.
22.   Having decided not to go any further that day, we put up at the nearest hotel.
23.   Failing your help I must try to carry out my task alone.
24. . To add to his difficulties, his partner died.
25.   He was horrified to see blood stains on the floor and no sign of his child.
26.   Besides men, women and children were also put to death.
27.   All except me went down to meet the train.
28.   In spite of his being a well-read man, in matters of business he is a fool.

29. Work at least six hours a day to make sure of success.
30. In spite of his being very poor, he does not complain..
31. Besides not returning the goods, he did not pay the bill.

EXERCISE 74

1. My friend having arrived, we went for a walk.
2. The servant having brought the lamp, I began my home-work.
3. The Ink having dried up, I could not write.
4. I have a lot of work to do now.
5. We must hurry to escape the rain.
6. He has an unpleasant duty to perform.
7. Besides pitying him, he relieved him.
8. He offended his master by doing this.
9. Having read the book carefully, he could tell the story in his own words.
10. His object becoming known, everybody tried to help him.
11. He was delighted at his good luck in finding a rupee.
12. Having hurt his ankle, Rama will not be able to play today.
13. Be good to be happy.
14. Not liking the work, he began it unwillingly.
15. He took no notice of my order to halt.
16. In spite of his being a good steady worker, he is rather slow.
17. In spite of my continually inviting him to visit me, he never came.
18. Having served out his sentence in gaol, he was released.
19. Being a good obedient boy, he worked exceedingly hard at school.
20. The dacoits having stopped to divide the booty, the police overtook him.
21. Practising daily, he became an expert player.
22. Having had no good result, your attempt can hardly be successful.
23. The Viceroy coming into the hall, everyone rose from his seat.
24. In spite of his escaping several times, he has finally been caught.
25. The horse falling heavily, his rider came down with him.
26. Finding himself getting weaker and weaker, he counsulted a doctor.
27. The plague breaking out in the city, the people moved out into the jungle.
28. Having no money with me, I could not give the beggar anything.

EXERCISE 75

1. I expect that I shall meet Rama tonight.
2. He hoped that he would win the prize.
3. It is not likely that his father will punish him.
4. He admitted that he had stolen the watch.
5. Krishna wishes that I should play for his team.

6. He believes that their success is certain in that case.
7. I overheard all that he remarked
8. I did not think that it would be fit to reply to his writings.
9. He confessed that he had committed a fault.
10. Where he is hiding is still unknown.
11. I shall be glad if you advise me in this matter.
12. He pleaded that he was ignorant of the law.
13. Our friends will hear that we have succeeded.
14. You imply by your words and manner that I am guilty.
15. I request that you should help me.
16. I cannot foretell when I shall depart.
17. I wish you would be quiet.
18. It is said that he is a millionaire.
19. Tell what is true.
20. I have long suspected that he is poor.

EXERCISE 76

1. I saw a bird that was wounded.
2. Rama is happy in the class where he is at present.
3. The man who is near me is my brother.
4. Our guru is a man who leads a blameless life.
5. Your father is the man who can help you in this matter.
6. The value which exercise has is great.
7. Was this the deed that a good man would do?
8. I was the first who heard the news.
9. These are not the methods which are adopted in business.
10. The class-room is not the place where boys can play.
11. He is hardly the boy that can do credit to the school.
12. He liked the place where he lived (or : worked) formerly.
13. Smoke, which is the certain indicator of fire, appeared in the mine.
14. I was the first who arrived.
15. That is not the way in which it should be answered.
16. It was the work which was done by a wild animal.
17. He is the man who carries water.
18. I have no place where I can sit.
19. My friend, who is the magistrate of this place, is on leave.
20. He sat outside on a stone which was in the compound.

EXERCISE 77

1. When he was punished he wept.
2. When Queen Victoria was reigning there were many wars.
3. Since he was quite contented, he never grumbled.

4.   As he was ill-treated by his master, he ran away.
5.   He was so dull that he could not understand.
6.   The tiger is feared as it is fierce.
7.   If you permit me I will go away.
8.   The peon would be quite happy if he was paid another rupee a month.
9.   He replied as well as he could.
10. I can only tell you as far as I remember.
11. Rama works harder than Krishna does.
12. As his health is bad, he has resigned.
13. He was annoyed when he was rebuked.
14. He cannot be caught as he is quick.
15. He is so lazy that he cannot succeed.
16. He came in very quickly so that he might avoid waking his father.
17. He waited there so that he might meet me.
18. One cannot be admitted unless one has permission.
19. I will help you as I can.
20. Do not go out unless you get leave.
21. Though it was hot, they marched quickly.
22. Though he is young, he is very capable.
23. Wait here till I arrive.
24. After his father died, he left Bombay.
25. Until he was thirty he remained unmarried.
26. Since he had that illness he has been partly blind.
27. Before he died he made his will.
28. As I anticipate sanction I have issued the order.
29. He hindered the police when they were executing their duty.
30. This was done when I was absent.
31. They kept silent lest they should be imprisoned.
32. He shot the dog though I entreated him not to do so.
33. He wrote as he was instructed.
34. He worked as well as he could.
35. Come back when it is six o'clock.
36. The body quivered every time when a blow was given.
37. If I am to speak honestly , I do not know.
38. I came today so that I might take advantage of the special train.
39. I was greatly surprised that he failed.
40. Till the day of examination arrived he did no more work.
41. When the tiger had fallen, he climbed down from the tree.
42. When Aurangzeb ruled, taxes were very heavy.
43. We eat that we may live.
44. Some people live so that they may eat.
45. He has gone down to the river so that they may bathe.
46. Have you come that you may see me?
47. Does he wish that I should go?

EXERCISE 78

1. Can you tell me when he will arrive?
2. After he saw the Chief Minister he departed.
3. Many ships were so shattered that they were wholly unmanageable.
4. England expects that every man will do his duty.
5. When the guests departed, he went to bed.
6. Few know the date when Lucy died.
7. It was difficult to discover where the source of the Nile was.
8. I will meet you at any place that is convenient for you.
9. Though he eanestly protested, he was condemned.
10. He is proud that he was born of a high family.
11. The prince was to be found where the battle was the hottest.
12. I rejoice that he has good fortune.
13. If he had not confessed it himself, the crime could scarcely have been brought home to him.
14. He alone entered, while the rest of us were waiting without.
15. As he was not feeling (or : did not feel) well, he decided to lie down.
16. As the last of these voyages did not prove very fortunate, I grew weary of the sea.
17. If we consider the difficulties of his position, he has acted admirably.
18. Speak low so that you may prevent our being overheard.
19. He was so much excited that he could not hear reason.
20. A letter from the butler brings to the club the news that Sir Roger is dead.
21. There is none who can dispute my right.
22. As he was accustomed to rule, he schooled himself to obey.
23. He saved the child though it risked his life.
24. A tree that is good cannot bring forth evil fruit.
25. I convinced him that he was mistaken.
26. It all depends upon how you do it.
27. He can prove that he is innocent.
28. Everybody knows who the author of Gulliver's Travels is.
29. The date when he will arrive is uncertain.
30. How long the war will last is uncertain.
31. There is no hope that he will recover.
32. The exact date when Buddha was born is unknown.
33. If one wants to maintain perfect health, one should have a daily bath.
34. Success or failure depends largely on the efforts you make.
35. As I was in a hurry I forgot the most important letters.
36. Those who listen never hear any good of themselves.
37. Finding that the door was unlocked, the thief entered the house.
38. It is impossible to trust the word of one who is a habitual liar.

39. Gray, who is the author of the Elegy, lived in the eighteenth century.
40. The shepherd found the sheep that was lost.
41. The boy readily admitted that he had made the mistake.
42. Tell me what your plans are.
43. He could clearly remember the incidents that occurred in his youth.
44. When he arrived at the foot of the hill, he blew his trumpet.
45. It was a spider that saved Robert Bruce.
46. The man that is prudent looks to the future.
47. As he had no money, he was unable to prosecute his studies.
48. As all the money had been spent, we started looking for work.
49. Those who are idle cannot hope to succeed.
50. Our orders were that we should show no mercy.
51. It was so late that they could not retreat.
52. I must be cruel that I may be kind.
53. The men fought as they were in desperation.
54. He is so truthful that he cannot be a successful courtier.
55. What you will be paid depends on the quality of your work. (or : The remuneration which you will get depends on the quality of your work.)
56. He conducted himself madly so that he might escape suspicion.
57. Good boys need not fear that they will be punished.
58. The accused confessed that he was guilty.
59. I asked him why he had come.
60. If it had not been for your folly, you could have been a partner in the firm today.
61. Tell me what your age is, (or : Tell me how old you are.)
62. I was glad when I heard of your arrival (or : I was glad to hear that you had arrived.)
63. As he was a very diligent and clever lad, he soon distinguished himself.
64. He is so short that he is not fit to be a soldier.
65. It was said that this is the birthplace of Budha.
66. His success went beyond what he expected.
67. Though he was in poor health, he worked hard.
68. As he felt out of sorts, he went to bed.
69. He complained that he had been unjustly treated.
70. He killed the hen so that he might get the treasure.
71. An army of ants will attack animals which are large and ferocious.
72. A planter who was very miserly formerly lived in the island of Jamaica.
73. He often gave his poor slaves food that was too little.
74. If you are industrious, you will be kept from want.
75. A man that is drowning will catch at a straw.
76. It is excellent to have the strength that a giant has.
77. When we finished our work, we went out for a walk.
78. Though thou hast thy faults I love thee still.

79.   The news is so good that it cannot be true.
80.   This tree is so high that I cannot climb it.
81.   He is so old that he cannot learn anything new.
82.   The world's greatest men have not laboured so that they may become rich.
83.   When the wind changes, we shall have rain.
84.   Though he has great wealth, he is not happy.

EXERCISE 79

1.   We believe in his innocence.
2.   His absence was much regretted.
3.   The consequence of his carelessness was the loss of the game.
4.   He asked the reason of my coming.
5.   He ordered the execution of the traitor.
6.   His escaping unhurt is to be hoped for.
7.   I do not know the time of my return.
8.   We hope for better times to come.
9.   The news of the landing of the enemy spread like wild fire.
10. My success does not make me happy.
11. He ordered the police to imprison the rioters.
12. Your willingness to believe this is incredible.
13. A prudent person is respected.
14. The victory of our troops is reported.
15. All believed him to be guilt of murder.
16. Tell me your meaning.

EXERCISE 80

1.   He sold his brother's horse.
2.   Being unable to help in any other way, I gave her some money.
3.   I have no horse to lend you.
4.   The marks left by whip were still visible.
5.   This is our camping place.
6.   The heart full of grief is heavy.
7.   Your reply is foolish.
8.   The evil done by men lives after them.
9.   Do you not remember him, your former friend?
10. This is her knitting needle.
11. Have you nothing to say?
12. He prospered by the help of his friends.
13. They were advised by a clever lawyer, a High Court pleader.
14. He is weak from his recent illness.
15. A dead man needs to riches.

16. I have seen Rama's house.
17. He was the most learned of the judges of that time.
18. He died in his native village.
19. The horse, being an Arab of pure blood, is very swift.
20. The smell coming from this drain is very bad.
21. Can he get no work to do?
22. Is there no place for bathing here?
23. The birds have no water to drink.
24. He shot a tiger, the scourge of the district.
25. That is my book.
26. I saw a blind man.
27. This is the water-bottle.
28. The chief achievement of Wycliffe and his friends was the translation of the Bible into Enlgish.
29. I found the lost book.
30. The boy standing first got the prize.
31. A city on a hill cannot be hid.
32. People living in glass houses must not throw stones.
33. His services to the state cannot be over estimated.
34. Their dwelling place is very unhealthy.
35. This basic idea of his philosophy is very difficult to comprehend.
36. I have no time to waste on idle talk.
37. A person relying on his own efforts has the best chance to win success.
38. Here is an impassable barrier.
39. A self-made man is always respected.
40. A notoriously idle boy was awarded a prize.
41. Men like you cannot be easily disheartened.
42. An industrious man is sure to succeed.
43. He told us the expected time of his arrival.

EXERCISE 81

1. Being here, you may as well see it.
2. He was angry to hear the result.
3. Does he know the consequences of his refusal?
4. He cannot go without my consent.
5. In the event of your talking always, you cannot always talk sense.
6. You never come here but to steal something.
7. The boy ran at his highest speed.
8. It beginning to rain, we waited a while.
9. In spite of his having failed twice, he will try again..
10. He made such good speed as to be in time.

11. Because of his illness, he stayed at home.
12. Feeling cold, he lit a fire.
13. Being unable to get much, I accept little.
14. He will pay you on hearing from you.
15. He was too tired to sleep.
16. They rejoice at their going.
17. I congratulated him on his passing.
18. Being rich, he can afford to be generous.
19. The hour having arrived, they started.
20. Believing his word, I did not ask for proof.
21. Seeing the cat, the dog jumped up.
22. The horse is too old to walk.
23. The tiger is renowned through all the countryside for his cunning and ferocity.
24. He was very angry at having to pay again.
25. Darkness increases in proportion to the period of our waiting here.
26. He is not too tall to enter the doorway.
27. Hearing the signal, they sprang up.
28. The truth being known, further lying is useless.
29. Everywhere I shall follow you.
30. Immediately on seeing us he disappeared.
31. Immediately on hearing the news he wrote to me.
32. I shall punish you for this act.
33. In his absence I spoke to his father.
34. They went to a cheaper place to live in.
35. Everywhere the people gathered to listen to his preaching.
36. She stood like stone.
37. We have come to help you.
38. You will pass by working hard.
39. He cannot see without wearing glasses.
40. His father still trusted him in spite of his deceit.
41. He is not prudent enough.
42. It was too dark to see your hand.
43. The fraud being discovered, he was imprisoned after trial.
44. He was too indolent to be successful.
45. An honest boy speaks out his thoughts.
46. Sit down anywhere.
47. The vigour of the mind increases in proportion to the size of the brain.
48. I shall give you my horse in exchange for your silver.
49. We will do the work to the best of our ability.
50. Robinson Crusoe was puzzled to discover the print of a foot on the sand.
51. He will not be frightened even at the fall of the sky.
52. Apollo was worshipped throughout the period of the Roman Empire.

53. I will buy it at any cost.
54. I am surprised at your believing such nonsense.
55. I will support all your acts.

EXERCISE 82

1. It is terrible for people to die of starvation.
2. I was unable to hear your words.
3. The weather being too stormy, we did not go.
4. His success is doubtful.
5. He became too ill to walk.
6. No one is promoted to a higher class without being examined.
7. He ran at his highest speed.
8. He promised to come tomorrow.
9. Tell me the place of your residence.
10. He confessed his guilt.
11. It was dark enough for us to lose our way.
12. Tell me your age.
13. The time of his arrival is not yet known.
14. Grant me my request.
15. We hope for better times to come.
16. I insist on your not going.
17. I shall remain in my place.
18. Turning to the right, you will soon reach the temple.
19. He gave a graphic account of his escape.
20. We went half-an-hour earlier so as to get a good seat.
21. He complained of unjust treatment.
22. He is certain to come. (or : He will certainly come.)
23. The Commissioner gave reward to deserving men.
24. I asked him the reason for his coming.
25. An orphan child is to be pitied.
26. To catch the early train they left at six o'clock.
27. Suspicion always haunts the mind of a guilty person.
28. He went to Ooty to improve his health.
29. A book containing pictures of animals was presented to him by his uncle.
30. Seeing Brutus among the assassins, he covered his face with his gown.
31. John Bright once spoke of a first-class carriage in an express train as the safest place in England.
32. The question is too complicated to be settled immediately.
33. But for his absence, the motion would have been carried.
34. The passage is too difficult for me to comprehend.
35. We must do the work to the best of our ability.
36. In spite of their most valiant fight, they were defeated.
37. In the event of his winning the battle, he will be crowned.

38. I wish to know the time of his death.
39. The surviving soldiers have received medals.
40. This is a sewing machine.
41. He seemed very anxious for us to come.
42. The priests were satisfied with his offer of the money.
43. You must be hungry in the event of your not having denied.
44. It is time for you to go.
45. Luckily, he came just then.
46. He is certain to help you. (or : He will certainly help you.)
47. You must write to me immediately on reaching Mumbai.
48. He gave away some books belonging to his brother.
49. Can you tell me the name of the author of the book?
50. He is said to have won by his own effort.
51. I cannot come in my parents' absence.
52. This sum is too hard for me to do.
53. One man falling, another took his place.
54. Work as hard as possible.
55. Drink while possible.
56. A man like him should succeed.
57. The police know this from information received by them.

EXERCISE 83

1. If you spare the rod, you will spoil the child.
2. After he put on his hat, he went outside.
3. When she woke at length she looked around.
4. If you do not keep quiet, you will be punished.
5. Though the ship was wrecked, the crew were saved.
6. If Shirin does not come, she will send a letter.
7. If you do your best, you will never reject it.
8. As soon as he received your telegram, he set off.
9. If I do not hurry back at once, my business will greatly suffer.
10. Unless you do this, you will be punished.
11. Though Rama may not be clever, he is certainly industrious.
12. After I put my hand into my pocket I gave him ten paise.
13. If you do the right, you will have no reason to be ashamed.
14. The crow, when he had stolen a piece of cheese, few with it to a tree.
15. When I called at your house yesterday, you were out.
16. Since this is the prisoner's first offence, he will be let off with a small fine.
17. If we do not do our work well, our master will be angry with us.
18. Since you have earned his gratitude, you will not go unrewarded.
19. After he failed in his first attempt, he never tried again.

20. Though time flies fast, it sometimes appears to move slowly.
21. It is well-known that mosquitoes cause malaria.
22. If she does not weep, she will die.
23. Though he ran to the station, he missed the train.
24. As the boy was tired, he went to bed.
25. Though he is poor, he is contented.
26. Though life has few enjoyments, we cling to it.
27. If you eat few suppers, you will need few medicines.
28. As he is working hard, he will succeed.
29. He works hard so that he may succeed.
30. While he was going along this road, he met a dragon.
31. Though they were refused pay, they went on working.
32. Though I frowned upon him, he loves me still.
33. If you find victories, we will find rewards.
34. Though, the arches were poorly armed, they offered a stubborn resistance.
35. If you cross this line, you will be captured.
36. Unless you are warmly clad, you will catch cold.
37. If you take care of his pence, the pounds will take care of themselves.
38. Though the Knight adored his proud wife, he was in mortal fear of her fierce temper.
39. Though we are few, we are of the right sort.
40. If you are diligent, you will succeed.
41. Though it seems too good to be true, it is a fact.
42. If you resist the devil, he will flee from you.
43. If I fail to recover it, I will die in the attempt.
44. If you take a farthing from a hundred pounds, it will be a hundred pounds no longer.
45. He has lost all his teeth so that he cannot eat hard food.
46. If you give him an inch, he'll take an ell.
47. If you hear him out, you will understand him the better.
48. If you advance another step, you are a dead man.
49. If you send the deed after me, I will sign it.
50. As he was very learned, he seemed to know everything.
51. As he was ambitious, I killed him.
52. After we landed at Karachi, we spent there a very enjoyable week.
53. When he called upon Mr. Pundit, he introduced us to his partner.
54. As he was my friend, I loved him.

EXERCISE 84

1. If you give me the book I will read it.
2. If you take quinine, your fever will be cured.
3. When I tell him to be quiet he takes no notice.

4. Though he is deaf, he will always pretend to hear.
5. Though you have paid the bill, you will get no more credit.
6. Though I ran all the way to the station, I missed the train.
7. Since Rama is a better player than Krishna, he must take his place in the team.
8. As you called me, I am here.
9. As the master is nearly blind, the boys are very sorry for him.
10. If we do not win, we shall die.
11. If you do not let me come in, I will break down the door.
12. If you are careful in your diet, you will keep healthy.
13. If you listen I will tell you all.
14. Though he is very agreeable, I don't like him.
15. As it is cold, I shall wear a coat.
16. If you send me the gun, I will mend it.
17. If you are good, you need not be clever.
18. If you do not follow me, you will lose your way.
19. As you ordered the goods, they have been sent.
20. If you do not pay, sign a chit.
21. As I don't like his lectures, I don't attend them.
22. If he had not run away, they would have killed him.
23. Though he has injured me, I will forgive him.
24. If you are not quiet, I shall punish you.
25. If you are just, you need not fear.
26. Though he was never present, he always sent a deputy.
27. Be so kind that you will help me.
28. If you pay heed to the small details, the general plans will surely succeed.
29. Since he is certain to be late, why wait for him?
30. If you do not go away, I must.
31. As the Parsis went in first on a very wet wicket, they lose the match.
32. Though they tried to bribe the peon, he was too clever for them.

EXERCISE 85

1. Once upon a time a man owned a hen and it laid every day a golden egg.
2. We tried several bicycles and then selected this.
3. He did not succeed and this is surprising.
4. Take exercise, or you will be ill.
5. Run and you will be in time.
6. He was afraid and therefore ran away.
7. He was not there and therefore I spoke to his brother.
8. He saw the danger, yet he pressed on.
9. You may try with all your might, but you will not succeed.
10. I must be invited, or I shall not go.

11. Don't eat too much or you will be ill.
12. There may be nothing in it, still it is a book.
13. Keep quiet, or you will be punished.
14. Casear loved me and so I weep for him.
15. You have done this and so I will punish you.
16. He heard the news and at once he wrote to me.
17. Rest and then go on with the work.
18. He was dying and therefore I forgave him.
19. He was feeling ill and therefore he stayed at home.
20. He had deceived him, yet his father trusted him.
21. The sky may fall, but he will not be frightened.
22. He was educated at a public school and there he learnt Latin.
23. He ventured to obstruct my path, so I struck him.
24. They wished to extend their empire and therefore they went to war.
25. They fought most valiantly, but they were defeated,
26. He writes very illegibly and so I cannot read his letter.
27. You told him something and I know it.
28. The ship was steered very successfully and so it reached the harbour safely.
29. Be respectable and you will be respected.
30. He was ambitious and therefore I killed him.
31. She was often capricious and impertinent, yet she was never out of temper.
32. The waves are raging white, but yet I'll row you o'er the ferry.
33. He began late, but finished first.
34. He tries hard, but he is seldom successful.
35. The sun set and he returned home.
36. Duty calls us and we must obey.
37. He had a cow and it gave enormous quantities of milk.
38. He was too rash and therefore failed.
39. We wish to live and so we eat.
40. He was very learned and seemed to know everything.

EXERCISE 86

1. Rama finished his meal and went to school.
2. I ask a civil question and expect a civil reply.
3. They opened the shop and they have not been poor ever since.
4. I can answer, but I don't choose to.
5. We may not be able to admire a weak man, but we might admire a bad one.
6. You may not succeed, yet I advise you to try.
7. You should understand, so I spoke plainly.
8. He feigned sleep, for he had an object in doing so.
9. Fight was useless and therefore he gave himself up.

10. We are here and so we will stay here.
11. He will not come and I think so.
12. There is a rupee in your hand and I know it.
13. Come at any time and you have option in the matter.
14. I must be in better health and then I shall come.
15. I did not see the snake, so I did not shoot it.
16. His practice is disgraceful, yet his precept is equally beautiful.
17. We may be at Rome and there we must behave as Romans do.
18. I fired and he fell.
19. Come here and you will repent it.
20. He left Mumbai and I have not heard from him ever since.
21. He wished to leave a message and therefore went to the hourse.
22. We must run, or we shall miss the train.
23. The sun touches the horizon and immediately darkness begins to settle upon the scene.
24. You may be very clever, yet you cannot succeed without industry.
25. Do this, or a worse thing will befall.
26. Trust to the book and you will find yourself in difficulties.
27. We should keep our honour sustained and we may lose all without regret.
28. Things are bad and they might be worse.
29. Finish your work and then you may go.
30. His bite is bad, but his bark is worse.
31. Either I am right or you are.

EXERCISE 87

1. No sooner did the ship touch the shore than a soldier of the tenth legion leaped into the water.
2. We have helped them not only with money but also with a body of workers, all well-trained and experienced.
3. Mrs. Smith is wiser than any other member of the family and Jane is prettier than any of her other three daughters.
4. A special service devised for the occasion helped solve the difficulty.
5. The doctor compelled the lady to drink such vile medicine that he all but killed her with it.
6. These affairs are already as well known to you as to me.
7. No sooner had Sir Roger seated himself than he called for wax candles.
8. When the preparation of supper was over, Robinson Crusoe sat down in expectation of enjoying himself greatly.
9. Nelson knew the value of obedience too well not to anticipate some censure for his act.
10. The secretary did not reply me for ten days.
11. If you have a look at the newspaper, you will find a lot of space devoted to advertisements.

12. She had no money; therefore she did not go with us.
13. He has not only a salary but also a private income.
14. Poverty compelled his parents to send him abroad to earn his own living.
15. The more proficient he becomes in games, the fonder he grows of them.
16. Of all the men known to me none is less inclined than he is to believe ill of others. (or : Of all the men I know he is the least inclined to believe ill of others.)
17. At the break of the monsoon the temperature had a rapid fall.
18. He has not only squandered his fortune and estranged his friends, but also ruined his health by his recklessness and extravagance.
19. The new facts he has discovered and the new arguments he has advanced have not changed my opinion.
20. (1) His treatment of his servants is notoriously mean.
    (2) He treats his servants in a notoriously mean way.
    (3) It is notorious that he treats his servants meanly.
    (4) The meanness with which he treats his servants is notorious.
21. You can imagine how annoyed I was when I learnt that the football match had been postponed.
22. He has no income other than what he earns by his pen.
23. (1) It was a sailing ship that was wrecked here last December.
    (2) It was here that a sailing ship was wrecked last December.
    (3) It was last December that a sailing ship was wrecked here.
24. There is a probability of his coming back.

EXERCISE 88

1. Having hurt his foot, he stopped.
2. Having been in prison before, the thief received severe sentences.
3. Unwilling to go any further, he returned home.
4. Seeing the uselessness of violence, they changed their policy.
5. (Being) weary of failure, he emigrated to Africa.
6. (Being) warned of his danger, he made good his escape.
7. Losing a large sum of money, he gave up speculation.
8. Receiving no answer, I knocked a second time.
9. His wife having encouraged him (or : Encouraged by his wife), he presevered.
10. Not satisfied with his salary, he gave up his situation.
11. Feeling tired, he laid his work aside.
12. Seeing Hari on the path, he went straight on.
13. The stable door being open, the horse was stolen.
14. Taking up his gun, he went out to shoot the lion.
15. I went to Mumbai last year to see a dentist.
16. Stealing a piece of cheese, a crow flew to her nest to enjoy the tasty meal.
17. Taking pity on the mouse, the magician turned it into the cat.

18. Alighting from the train, a passenger fell over a bag on the platform.
19. Charmed with the silk, my sister bought ten yards.
20. I did not hear his answer, it being spoken quietly. (Or : Spoken quietly, his answer was not heard by me.)
21. (Being) delayed by a storm, the steamer came into a port a day late.
22. Having resolved on a certain course, he acted with vigour.
23. The letter being badly written, I had great difficulty in making out its contents.
24. A hungry fox saw some bunches of grapes hanging from a vine.
25. Hurrying away with much haste, Cinderella dropped one of her little glass-slippers.
26. Walking along the street one day, I saw a dead snake.
27. Being overpowered, he surrendered.
28. Running at top speed, he got out of breath.
29. Possessing all the advantages of education and wealth, he never made a name.
30. (Being) occupied with important matters, he had no leisure to see visitors.
31. The Russians having burnt Moscow, the French were forced to quit it.
32. The votes on the each side being equal, the chairman gave his casting vote against the resolution.
33. Losing the favour of his master, Wolsey was dismissed from his high offices.
34. Being a big and very strong boy, he is in the football team.
35. Being ill, he came to me for leave.
36. I heard Abdul shouting very loudly, and calling me.
37. Raising his gun and taking aim, he shot the tiger.
38. Being very old and having lost his teeth, he could not eat hard food.
39. Having told you the facts and having nothing more to say, I will sit down.
40. Returning home, I saw a man looking very ill and lying by the roadside.

EXERCISE 89

1. There goes my brother Sohrab.
2. The cow provides milk, a valuable food.
3. Mr. Pundit, a well-known Sanskrit scholar, was elected President.
4. Coal, a very important mineral, is hard, bright, black, and brittle.
5. We saw the picture, a very fine piece of work.
6. Geoffrey Chaucer, the first great English poet, was born in 1340.
7. Tagore's most famous work is the Gitanjali, a collection of short poems.
8. His only son, a lad of great promise, died before him.
9. His uncle, a millionaire, sent him to England for his education.

10. The dog bit the man, a notorious burglar.
11. I love my faithful dog Bruno.
12. Jawaharlal Nehru, the first Prime Minister of India, died in 1964.
13. De Lesseps, a French engineer, made the Suez Canal, a great work.
14. Mr. Pundit, the Collector, lives in Dustipur, a large town.

EXERCISE 90

1. He earned promotion by attending to his duties.
2. He may escape punishment by confessing his fault.
3. On account of his illness last term, he was unable to attend school.
4. My forgiving him his fault has not prevented him from repeating it.
5. At the sound of the bugle the weary soldiers leapt to their feet.
6. At the word of command you will fire.
7. By setting traps every night he cleared his house of rats.
8. The court listened silently to the decision given by the judge.
9. In expectation of obtaining leave he has already bought his steamer ticket.
10. It is impossible to suspect a man with such a good record.
11. Even a bird shows great courage in defending its young ones.
12. For a want of provisions the garrison could hold out no longer.
13. But for your help I should have been drowned.
14. On examining the statement I find many errors in it.
15. At least in appearance he is free from disease.
16. He never fully recovered from the shock of his son's death.
17. He was not justified in taking the law in his own hands.
18. The streets were flooded by the heavy rain.
19. In spite of his heroic efforts to succeed, he failed.
20. The weather is pleasant in spite of its being a little cold.
21. I took no notice of its rudeness.
22. There is no doubt about his having stolen the purse.
23. Her father is opposed to her marrying a foreigner.
24. I was surprised at his entering the room with his hat on (or : To my surprise he entered the room with his hat on.)
25. He got great honour by saving the life of the Rajah.
26. His interest was aroused by an advertisement in the newspaper.
27. He amused us very much by singing a funny song.
28. On hearing of the prince's illness the people crowded to the place.
29. On receiving the news of the recovery of the prince, the people were very enthusiastic.
30. He makes a lot of money by buying and selling horses.
31. I saw a sowar with a lance in his hand and a sword by his side.
32. She stood there for hours without moving or speaking.
33. The discovery of his crime was a heavy blow to his reputation and his business,

EXERCISE 91

1. His friend having arrived, he was very pleased.
2. The rain having fallen, the crops revived.
3. The storm having ceased, the sun came out.
4. The troops having been ordered out, the police were unable to hold the mob in check.
5. The holidays being at an end, boys are returning to school.
6. The wind having failed, the crew set to work with a will.
7. It being a very hot day, I could not do my work satisfactorily.
8. His house having been burned down, he lives in a hotel.
9. The King having died, his eldest son came to the throne.
10. His father being dead, he had to support his widowed mother.
11. Rain having been plentiful this year, rice is cheap.
12. The secretaryship being vacant and nobody being willing to undertake duties of the post, I offered my services.
13. The prisoner being questioned and no witness coming forward, the judge dismissed the case.
14. The sun having risen and the fog having cleared away, the lighthouse was seen less than a mile away.
15. He having fired his gun and the ball having gone high, the tiger sprang on him.
16. The master being out of the room and the door being shut, the boys made a lot of noise.

EXERCISE 92

1. He had no money to give away.
2. I have nothing more to tell you.
3. He is too poor to afford a motor-car.
4. I was glad to hear of his good fortune.
5. The information has come too late to be of any use to us.
6. Your father will be delighted to hear of your success.
7. You were prudent not to invest all your savings in one concern.
8. He had not even ten paise with him to buy a loaf of bread.
9. The Pathan took out a knife to frighten the old man.
10. I am not afraid to speak the truth.
11. He works hard to earn his livelihood.
12. The strikers held a meeting to discuss the terms of the employers.
13. He has five children to support for.
14. Napolean is universally acknowledged to have been one of the greatest of generals.
15. Various means were employed by His Majesty to kill Gulliver secretly.
16. I will not be afraid to speak the truth.

17. He is honourable enough not to break his word.
18. He has some bills to pay.
19. He must apologize to escape punishment.
20. He keeps some fierce dogs to guard his house and keep away robbers.

EXERCISE 93

1. I accept your statement unreservedly.
2. He answered me correctly.
3. He forgot his umbrella carelessly.
4. He is certainly a bad boy.
5. The train is usually very late.
6. I shall come back soon.
7. He kicked the goal-keeper intentionally.
8. He obstinately refused to listen to advice.
9. He spent all his money foolishly.
10. He was unavoidably absent at the meeting.
11. He applied for leave unsuccessfully.
12. He admitted his error regretfully.
13. I met him only once in a railway carriage.
14. He has succeeded unexpectedly.
15. It must be done at any cost.
16. I have read Bacon to my great profit.
17. He preserved indomitably.
18. The door was rather suspiciously open.
19. He is not qualified for the post in any degree.
20. The blow dazed him only for a time.
21. Luckily, I did not eat any of the poisoned food.
22. He solved the problem in no time.
23. He visited Ooty for reasons of health.
24. He accomplished the task with unflogging industry.
25. Boys grow up to be men slowly and imperceptibly.
26. Rama struck Krishna cruelly, frequently and unreasonably.

EXERCISE 94

1. Nobody knows the birth-place of the great poet Homer.
2. Being a leader, he did not naturally follow other men.
3. This hat, bought by me two years ago, is still good and fit to wear.
4. For thirty years he devoted himself to public affairs without taking a holiday.

5.   Clive's proposals, in spite of opposition by some, were carried with the support of the majority.

6.   Clive informed the council of his determination to introduce necessary reforms in the administration.

7.   The man, in spite of his innocence and his ability to defend himself, refused to speak for fear of convicting his friend.

8.   While in prison, he was able to talk to his friend in the next cell by making a hole in the brick wall between the cells.

9.   A workman, hearing the shouts of the drowning boy for help, plunged into the river at the risk of his-own life.

10. The traveller, toiling slowly over the desert, suddenly turned turned round on hearing his companion crying for help.

11. Returning down the valley of the Jumna, we came first to Delhi, the capital of India.

12. The art of printing was introduced into England during the reign of Edward IV by William Caxton, a native of Kent.

13. Striking his foot against a stone, he fell to the ground making his clothes, very dirty.

14. The corn having ripened in the sun in a short time, the farmer was filled with joy.

15. Opening his letters, reading them carefully and sending for his clerk, he dictated answers to them.

16. His payment of all his late father's debts, a very honest proceeding, was very creditable to him.

17. He has two horses to feed, water, groom and bring to his master at 12 o'clock.

18. He goes to school to learn and grow up honest, healthy and clever.

19. My notice was drawn to a Pathan armed with a gun, hiding in my garden.

20. The soldiers starving, their ammunition being expended, their clothes being in rags and their leaders being dead, the enemy easily defeated them.

21. Inspired by Napolean, the first Emperor of the French and a great soldier, with the most war-like spirit, his armies won many victories.

22. Wellington, the greatest of English generals, Nelson, the greatest of English admirals, and Napolean, the greatest of French soldiers, were contemporary heroes of their respective countries.

23. Finding himself the richer by a paisa and seeing his adversary outwitted, the miser laughed.

24. He hardened his heart to punish the people mercilessly and make an example of them once and for all.

25. He receives much gratitude by performing kindly actions, by not being harsh in the execution of his duty and by not oppressing the poor.

26. His friends having assembled and offered him their congratulations upon his safe return and everybody being comfortably seated, he described all his adventures.

27. The thieves poisoned the dog brought from England and trained carefully to protect his property.

28. Vultures with cruel beaks and talons, appearing one after another and wheeling round and round, were descending towards the spot.

29. The room was covered with blood staining the walls and ceiling, darkening the floor, flowing in a stream under the door and standing in puddles everywhere.

30. The house having been pulled down, another having been built in its place, it was difficult to identify the exact spot.

31. He earned the hatred of all good men by inciting youths to crime, funishing them with means and keeping himself safely out of the way in time of danger.

32. He was punished for copying from the next boy, a mean and dishonest action bringing disgrace upon him.

33. He had not sufficient courage to face the opposition of his caste fellows or to go away from his native place to begin life afresh.

34. Rabindranath Tagore, a Nobel laureate and the author of the National Anthem, founded Shantiniketan.

35. Being very often ill and frequently absent, he had no opportunity to finish his work or to do much of it in fact.

36. He had often helped the criminal, a man of his own caste and an ungrateful and incorrigible wretch.

37. Picking up a wounded bird during a walk one day, bringing it home and tending it carefully for some time, he was very glad of its complete recovery.

38. A boy known to me at school is now famous as a soldier, known to the tribesmen as the "Sleepless One" and greatly feared by them.

39. The water being boiled, the tea being made, the food being ready and the table being spread, they sat down to eat and drink.

40. He deserves my thanks for having found my purse and returned it to me without taking anything from it.

41. I saw a terrier, a well-bred little animal with three legs and only one ear.

42. My orders to him were to clean all the silver, to put it away, to lock it up and to bring me the key of the box.

43. The horse had many of the points of a racer—slim legs, high withers, powerful quarters and a tremendous stride.

44. Having been a great statesman, having worked well for his country and having been very popular, he was accorded a tomb in Westminster Abbey.

45. Wood being collected, camp fires being lighted, food being cooked and eaten, the army lay down to sleep.

46. His conduct being disgraceful, he alienated himself, besides being put in gaol.

47. Rama with his wide knowledge of the business and Krishna with the necessary capital entered into partnership, combining resources.

48. Their father having divided his large sum of money equally between them by his will, the daughters were eagerly sought in marriage.

49. The ground, abounding in frogs and snakes, the enemies of mankind, is soft and marshy.
50. His superiors being pleased with him, he is justified in having high hopes.
51. He rode along for hours, without striking his horse or spurring it.
52. I have some advice to give you and impress strongly upon you.
53. I hear rumours about Laxman, an old pupil of mine, a good cricketer and a good football player but not a steady worker.
54. Delighted with the intelligence and brightness of the scholars, he overlooked the fact of their knowing few things by heart.
55. He built a house with many large doors, many large windows, wide verandahs and a general air of coolness and comfort.
56. He told a story about a famous warrior of great strength.
57. He came to Mumbai to see his father and settle some business.
58. The boat, having no mast after the storm and being unable to keep before the wind, could not return to port.
59. The cage strongly built for the purpose, contains a tiger.
60. The ancient myths of India have been preserved in the minds of the people with great care by the priests and the learned men, the guardians of the lamp of learning.

EXERCISE 95

1. He does well; only he is nervous at the start.
2. The way was long and the wind was cold.
3. It is raining heavily, so I will take an umbrella with me.
4. The harvest truly is plenteous, but the labourers are few.
5. It was a stormy night, yet we ventured out.
6. Football is a very vigorous and healthy game and therefore everybody should play it.
7. He is foolish and is also obstinate.
8. I am in the right, but you are in the wrong.
9. We can travel by land and can also travel by water.
10. The train was wrecked, but no one was hurt.
11. The paper is good, but the binding is very bad.
12. We must hasten, or the robbers will overtake us.
13. The prince married the beautiful princess and they lived happily ever after.
14. The river is deep and swift, so I am afraid to dive into it.
15. He was not only fined but also sent to prison.
16. You may go to the theatre and Rama also may.
17. Lying on his bed, Bruce looked up to the roof and saw a spider.
18. I cried out sadly, beat my head and breast and threw myself down on the ground.
19. You must play hockey, or you must play football.
20. Either you or Rashid is wrong and you cannot both be right.
21. I got up and looked about everywhere, but I could not perceive my companions.

22. In Hyderabad I visited Charminar, Golkonda Fort and Birla Mandir, but I could not visit Salar Jung Museum.

23. A is equal to B and B is equal to C and therefore A is equal to C.

24. Most of the rebels were slain and a few, having escaped, hid in the woods and marshes and thus the rebellion was quickly suppressed.

25. He was my school-fellow, but having become a great man, he has grown proud enough to forget his old friends.

26. I did not see you, but having important news, I should have spoken to you, for delay was dangerous.

27. Make haste or you will be late, for there is no other train till midnight and that train is a slow one.

28. Their boats are made of a kind of bark and they are light enough to be carried easily on the shoulders.

29. The emu, or Australian ostrich, does not sit on the eggs but covers them up with leaves and grass and leaves them to be hatched by the heat of the sun.

30. We must catch the 5 o'clock train and there being only half an hour left, we must start without further delay.

31. A timid dog is dangerous, for he always suspects ill-treatment and tries to protect himself by snapping.

32. A husbandman had sown some corn in his fields only recently and as cranes came to eat the corn, he fixed a net in his fields to catch them.

33. The monsoon having failed and the tanks having become almost empty, no grain could be sown and therefore a famine was feared and the ryots looked anxiously for the next monsoon, which, proving unusually abundant, averted the danger.

34. The second class carriage being full, we must either pay first class fare or wait for the next train, for we are forbidden to travel first class with second class tickets.

35. He is a rich man and, as he did not earn his wealth, he does not appreciate the value of money and squanders it.

36. He beat me in the race, for being a year older, he naturally runs faster, but next year I may do better.

37. The storm having abated, the sun shone, but the ship-wrecked mariners could see no sign of land and were adrift in the mid-ocean.

38. Generally your conduct is good and therefore you will not be punished for having been guilty of an act of folly, but I advise you to be more prudent in future.

39. Having lost my way, I asked a policeman to direct me, but being new to his work, he could not help me and called a gentleman passing by to my assistance.

40. Seeing the danger, the engine-driver applied the brakes, but as the line was greasy and the brakes failed to act quickly, the train crashed into the gates at the crossing and the engine left the rails.

41. The rain having fallen steadily for several days, the river overflowed its banks, so that the terrified villagers abandoned their homes and fled to the higher ground, but soon the floods retired and the villagers were able to return.

EXERCISE 96

1. I am sure that he is wrong.
2. His complaint was that you deceived him.
3. Do you know when the train will arrive?
4. I have often told you that all the planets except for Pluto travel round the sun the same way and in the same place.
5. It is certain that he will waste his time.
6. Tell me where you have put my hat.
7. In spite of the fact that he is short-tempered, I like him.
8. Ask the guard if it is time for the train to start.
9. I am sure that it is going to rain.
10. What is worth doing is worth doing well.
11. No one can doubt that he is a sincere worker.
12. I did not hear what he said.
13. Tell me how you found that out.
14. I think that you have made a mistake.
15. Can you tell me who wrote Shakuntala?
16. Do you deny that you stole the purse?
17. I cannot adequately express how sorry I am.
18. That we have been deceived is the truth.
19. It is a mystery how Netaji Subhash Chandra Bose died.
20. We expect that he will succeed.
21. Tell me what you have done.
22. We wished to know where we were going.
23. It was evident from the distant roar of water that we were nearing some waterfall.
24. We do not know how many of the enemies escaped.
25. I want to know why the two friends quarrelled.
26. The fact that he is a great orator cannot be denied,
27. I will show you how Columbus made an egg stand on its end.
28. I cannot remember where I have seen this man before.
29. I do not know when he will arrive.
30. It is difficult to understand why he distrusts his own sons.

EXERCISE 97

1. The man who committed the theft last night has been caught.
2. The French and the Italian languages are different forms of the Latin language, which was once spoken in almost every part to Europe.
3. The time when the accident happened was six o'clock.
4. Can you tell me the reason why you are not keeping good health lately?
5. All the plans which he has for earning money quickly have failed.
6. A lion who was proud of his strength despised the weakness of the mouse.

7. The fox saw the grapes which hung over the garden wall.
8. That is the school where I was taught.
9. Show me the place where you put it.
10. My travelling companion was an old gentleman by name Mr. Haq, whom I met in Basra.

EXERCISE 98

1. The nurse must be tired, as she had no sleep last night.
2. If a gentleman calls, please ask him to wait.
3. He ran so quickly that he soon overtook me.
4. Do not go till I get ready.
5. As he spoke in a very low voice, nobody could hear him.
6. Although I wound my watch this morning, it has stopped.
7. As it was very stuffy last night, I could not sleep last night.
8. Unless the monsoon breaks this month, the wells will run dry.
9. Whether I help you or not, you are sure to lose the game.
10. As soon as the fireman came out of the house, the roof collapsed.
11. Success attends hard work, while failure attends bad work.
12. If you do not hurry, you will miss the train.
13. When the delegates arrived, the discussion was resumed.
14. Though he is very old, he enjoys good health.
15. As no more funds are available, the work has been stopped.
16. As soon as he saw me coming, he took to his heels.
17. Though I am blunt, I am at least honest.
18. When he was contradicted he was annoyed.
19. As he bled profusely, he died.
20. Though it is true of some, it is not true of all.
21. As he ran quickly, he soon overtook me.
22. Your letter arrived after I had left home.
23. As soon as he saw us, he disappeared.
24. He will not go out in the rain lest he should get wet.
25. The bandits fought desperately, as they could not bear the idea of being taken alive.
26. The sailors cast anchor so that they might prevent the ship from drifting on the rocks.
27. Since you make a good deal of noise, I cannot work.
28. We may sail tomorrow if the weather permits.
29. It is so simple that even a child can understand it.
30. When he was returning from school, he was caught in a shower.
31. Robinson Crusoe was puzzled when he discovered the print of a foot on the sand.
32. When he finished the work, the clock just struck five.
33. Though he is being lionized, he keeps a level head.
34. Have you turned detective that you keep your eye on me like this?
35. After we travelled together as far as Calcutta, we parted company.
36. No other man in our community is as rich as he is.

37. Whether you wish to do the work or not, you must do it.
38. As he was sick, he remained at home.
39. If you have tears, prepare to shed them now.
40. Though he may slay me, I will trust him.
41. When he saw me he ran away.
42. He came to my house when I was out.
43. He has been very poor since his father died.
44. As he grew weaker and weaker , he died.
45. We take off our clothes when we go to bed.
46. He was hanged as he had committed murder.
47. All will respect you if you are honest.
48. He is so old that he cannot walk.
49. He won the race as he was the swiftest.
50. Let us be honest as long as life lasts.
51. The wolf is larger than the jackal is.
52. Arjun is as clever as Rama is.

EXERCISE 99

1. That is the man who gave me a dog that went mad.
2. That Rama will not play in the match is a foolish notion, as he is the best player in the school.
3. He praised me for writing the letter which contained truth.
4. Have you ever heard that honesty is the best policy.
5. He came to see me and tell me that his father was dead after having been ill for a long time.
6. The horse that I wished to sell you has killed the man who was trying to steal it.
7. When he took the medicine, he felt better as it cured his headache.
8. When he gave an order he was obeyed, as they fear to offend him.
9. As the absence of the girl from her home was unusual, inquiries were made, which led to no result.
10. I am not able to understand your conduct which has been described to me as very peculiar.
11. He played exceedingly well in the match yesterday so that his team won.
12. He told me that he had written a letter to his superior for a certain reason.
13. I visited his garden, where there were some beautiful rose-trees full of bloom, red and white in colour.
14. As no one would give him work, he forsook his dishonest ways, which had brought him to the depths of poverty.
15. Why does he worry since he is sure to receive his pay due to him?
16. He told me that the doctor who has attended him for years is not able to understand why he has very bad health though he lives very carefully.
17. Though his servants disliked him for his harshness, they flattered him.
18. I carefully sighted the rifle so as not to miss, since a miss might have cost me my life.

19. It should be kept in mind that the speed of the boast was remarkable though it was going against the current and the wind.

20. I was told that he stole a book in which was written the owner's name which was well known to him.

21. In order to surprise the enemy they had marched the whole journey, which was very long, at top speed.

22. Having got long leave, my friend is going to Europe, where his brother already is, so as to become a doctor.

23. Rama has declared it to be his intention not to play against the Hindu School, which has a very strong team, as he does not wish to tire himself before the cup-match, which takes place the next day.

24. It very often happens that the man who talks most does least.

25. Our father says that the man who did this must have been undoubtedly very strong.

26. I should like to know how much money he paid for the information, to whom and why, so that I can prosecute him.

27. Fearing pursuit and capture, they hid the very valuable treasure in some place in a jungle, which was never discovered.

28. It is not difficult to see the reason why he endeavoured to hide the traces of the crime that he had committed.

29. A man like him who had not learned to read and write, and who was very ignorant and could not even talk fluently, should not pretend to be a doctor.

30. The father fully described a large number of his boy's accomplishments to the teacher so that he might get him admitted to the school.

31. The jackal which was pursued by the dogs was caught, because it was very hungry while they were well fed.

32. Since he had ordered them to be punctual, he got more angry as he waited longer.

33. It is my duty to send you there, whether you like it or not.

34. If you wish to succeed as well as your father, you must work as hard as he did.

35. I am sorry to hear that you have failed, as I think that you deserved to pass.

36. The Principal has issued orders to the effects that you will be allowed to enter for the examination if you work hard.

37. Judging by the results of the examination, I think that Rama is cleverer than Krishna.

38. It is generally true that where there is a will there is a way.

39. Hearing the news, I went to the hospital, which is not far away from my house, to discover the extent of his injuries.

40. It is only right that he will promote you sooner or later according as you please him or displease him.

41. The proverb says that as you sow, so you will reap.

42. Wherever you look you will see signs of industry, which speak well for the prosperity of the people.

43. It is undeniable that the sight of a sword gives pleasure to a man like me, who has done much sword-play.

44. As they had been thoroughly well trained, they played the game at least as skilfully as anyone could have done.

45. His father was very grieved to receive the report that he was more idle and careless than the other boys in the school.

EXERCISE 100

1. When I offered him help which he needed, he persisted in refusing it, so I left him to his fate.

2. Toiling over the desert, a famished traveller was highly delighted to find a bag, but when he opened it he found nothing but pearls.

3. Hundreds of men and women have travelled in space, some for a few days and others for several months.

4. When I was in Sri Lanka in May last, I visited Mihintale, which is regarded as the cradle of Buddhism.

5. Once, as an oarsman was rowing by himself without looking behind him, he met another boat and crashed into it, so that he was upset.

6. A dog, while running away with a piece of meat, passed some deep still water and, seeing there the reflected image of meat, he dropped the meat into the deep water and snatched in vain at the shadow.

7. Seeing a crow sitting on a tree with a piece of cheese in his mouth, a fox praised his singing, and the crow, pleased by the flattery, began to sing so that he dropped the cheese.

8. When a lion, who was proud of his strength and despised the weakness of the mouse, was caught in a net and could not escape from it, he was set free by the exertions of the mouse.

9. Afraid of his barons, John, King of England, who did not care about liberty, signed a document called the Magna Carta at Runnymede on the Thames, not far from Windsor.

10. Running down the incline, the train attained great speed and, while turning a sharp curve at the bottom, it oscillated under the influence of the brakes and threw all the passengers into a panic.

11. Having managed to creep into a basket of corn, a half starved mouse rejoiced in his good fortune and fed greedily on the corn, but when he tried to get out of the basket, his body was too big to pass through the hole.

12. Venus and Mercury are nearer to the sun than the earth and, as they are very hot planets, it would not be possible for any life to survive on them.

13. A band of well-armed ruffians, some of whom were escaped convicts, entered a village at night, when the villagers were asleep, and stole their cattle.

14. While my fellow-traveller, who had a gun, was boasting of his bravery, a bear suddenly came behind a rock close in front of us and stood in our way, growling angrily.

15. Mungo Park, who was employed by the African Association, explored the interior regions of Africa and, the undertaking being hazardous, he suffered many distresses, which were often alleviated by the compassion of the negroes.

16. A lion, while drinking in a clear pool, saw his stately mane reflected by the pool and greatly admired it; but being afterwards pursued by hunters with their guns through a thick wood, he found his mane useless and of no avail.

17. As it was not possible to disobey the king who ordered me to go to a distant village, I set off for the village, where I was mortified to find no one willing to admit me into his house and, being regarded with astonishment and fear, I was obliged to sit the whole day without victuals while a tree protected me against the heat and the sun.

18. The wind rose and there were heavy rain clouds, so that the night was very threatening; and the wild beasts being numerous thereabout, to escape them it would have been necessary to climb a tree and sit among the branches.

19. The sun having set, I was preparing to pass the night in a tree, when a negro woman, who was returning from the labour of the field, stopped to observe me and, perceiving my weariness and dejection, inquired into my situation; and when I briefly explained it to her, with a look of compassion she told me to follow her.

20. She conducted me to her hut and told me to remain there for the night, and then, finding me hungry, she procured from outside a fine fish, caused it to be half-boiled upon some embers and gave it to me for supper.

21. He had made war on Saxony, set the Roman crown upon his head and become famous throughout the whole world, but his fame had not prevented his hair from becoming grey.

22. Being in his seventy-eighth year, having been reduced to despondency by the disaster in Germany, travelling at an unhealthy time of year and having exposed himself imprudently to the night air, Augustus probably died a natural death and all the other particulars are quite opposed to poison theory.

23. We enjoy the remotest products of the north and south and are free from extremities of the weather and our eyes are refreshed with the green fields of Britain, while our palates are refreshed with tropical fruits, which is not the least part of our happiness.

24. As he was treated very ungraciously by the court while being supported very enthusiastically by the people, it might be expected that he, being a man of haughty and vehement temper, would eagerly take the first opportunity of showing his power and gratifying his resentment.

25. Bonaparte, a Corsican by birth, having distinguished himself at school, joined the republican army as a corporal to start with, and by his remarkable bravery and great mental powers he became the head of the army of Italy, conquered Egypt, set aside the republic and was proclaimed Emperor.

26. Having been full of years and honours, he is now gone to his final reward, and those honours were especially dear to his heart, as they were gratefully bestowed by his pupils and bound him to the interests of that school, where he had been educated and to whose service his whole life had been dedicated.

EXERCISE 101

1. came 2. continued 3. spoke 4. knows 5. could 6. could 7. will 8. may 9. was 10. could 11. was 12. might 13. could 14. can 15. began 16. left 17. heard 18. was 19. meet 20. proceed 21. entered 22. felt 23. preached 24. were 25. was 26. choose 27. dared 28. could 29. can 30. could 31. might 32. were 33. was 34. repent 35. may 36. come 37. limped 38. like 39. might 40. lie 41. can 42. might 43. works 44. would 45. tried 46. could 47. expected 48. asked 49. could

EXERCISE 102

1.	might	2.	might	3.	may	4.	would	5.	can
6.	may/can	7.	might	8.	may	9.	could	10.	might
11.	can	12.	would	13.	might	14.	would	15.	could
16.	might	17.	could	18.	would	19.	might	20.	might
21.	would								

EXERCISE 103

1.	was	2.	were	3. ceased	4. sounded
5.	was	6.	gave	7. came/returned
8.	were	9.	had/been/was	10. is

EXERCISE 104

1. He reminded me that he had often told me not to play with fire.
2. The teacher remarked that they had all done it very badly.
3. They wrote that it was time they had thought about settling the matter.
4. The teacher promised that he would explain it if they would come before school the next day.
5. She wrote that she was waiting and watching and longing for her son's return.
6. The examiner's orders were that no one was to bring books into the room nor ask him questions about what he had told them to do.
7. The dwarf asked her to promise him that when she was Queen she would give him her first-born child.
8. He said that it was his horse and 'that if he did not prove it in a few minutes he would give up his claim.
9. He cried that he would avenge her/my wrongs and that he would not enter Athens until he punished the king who had so cruelly treated her/me.

10. He wrote and said that he was unable to come just then because he was ill, but he would certainly start as soon as he was well enough to do so.

11. One day he sent for Cassim and told him that he was then old enough to earn his living, so he had to set off and make his own way in the world.

EXERCISE 105

1. He asked her what she wanted.
2. He asked how my (her/his) father was.
3. He asked whether I (she/he) was going home with him.
4. He enquired when I (she/he) intended to pay him.
5. He asked us why we were all sitting about there doing nothing.
6. The prince asked whether I (she/he/we/they) really came from China.
7. The poor man exclaimed whether none of them would help him.
8. The young Raksha asked which way she had gone.
9. Aladdin asked the magician what he had done to deserve so severe a blow.
10. I asked whether he (she/they) did not know the way home.
11. He asked whether I (she/he) wrote a good hand.
12. The judge finally asked whether he (she) had anything to say on behalf of the prisoner.
13. The boy enquired of his father which the proper way to answer the question was.
14. Ulysses asked the bird whether it had anything to tell him.
15. The young sparrow asked its mother what that queer object was.
16. Then aloud he asked the boy to tell him whether the miller was within.
17. They asked who he was and what he wanted.
18. Stroking the bird's feathers, she asked affectionately whether it had come to comfort her in her sorrow.
19. The Rajah was deeply grieved and asked his wife what he could do for her.
20. When the sun got low, the king's son asked Jack where they could lodge that night, since they had no money.
21. She asked him what was it that made him so much stronger and braver than any other man.
22. When the Brahmin approached, the first thief asked why he carried a dog on his back and whether he was not ashamed.

EXERCISE 106

1. The swami asked the villagers to bring him a glass of milk.
2. The teacher told the boys to sit down.
3. The officer shouted to his men to halt.
4. The King ordered the Hatter to take off his hat.
5. The teacher advised him not to read so fast.
6. He asked me to wait until he came.
7. He told his servant to hurry up and not to waste time.
8. Their mother told the children to run away.

9.   He asked his daughter to take his golden jug and fetch him some water from the well.

10.   His master ordered him to go down to bazar and bring him some oil and a lump of ice.

EXERCISE 107

1.   Mr. Squeers exclaimed with a sigh that milk was, to be sure, a very rare article in London.

2.   He angrily remarked that I (he/she) was a very stupid fellow.

3.   He exclaimed sadly that he was ruined.

4.   He exclaimed sadly that their foes were too strong.

5.   He remarked that I/he was a very lazy boy and that I/he had done my/his work very badly.

6.   They exclaimed that they had passed the holiday merrily.

7.   He exclaimed that it was a nuisance.

8.   He remarked that it was very cruel of him.

9.   He exclaimed that it was a great pity I (she/he/they/we) had not come.

10.   The Queen exclaimed sadly that he had done a very rash and bloody deed.

EXERCISE 108

1.   He said to Rama, "Come with me."

2.   Rama replied, "I cannot do so."

3.   "When will the next letter come?" he said to his father.

4.   "There may not be another this year," replied his father.

5.   Rama said to me, "What has become of Hari?"

6.   "I have not seen him for months," I said to him.

7.   The master said, "Please attend carefully to what I am saying."

8.   I wrote, "I shall visit him tomorrow."

9.   He observed, "I have never liked doing that."

10.   "Be quiet" I said to them.

11.   "Have you anything to say?" he said to me.

12.   Rama said to Hari, "Will you change places with me?"

13.   "I am tired," he said. "I wish to go to bed."

14.   An old mouse said, "Who will bell the cat?"

15.   John said, "I want to be a soldier".

16.   "Where are you going?" he said to me.

17.   "What do you want?" he said to me.

18.   Abdul said, "I have seen this picture."

19.   The boy said, "I shall come with you."

20.   He said, "The earth moves round the sun."

21.   The stranger said to Alice, "Where do you live?"

22.   I said to Mary, "Will you lend me a pencil?"

23.   He said to us, "I have waited an hour."

24.   "Are you now quite well again?" the lady inquired.

25.   He said, "I have come to see you."

26. He said, "Even though I have come, it is against my will."
27. The speaker said, "It gives me great pleasure to be here this evening."
28. He said to them, "Will you listen to such a man?"
29. He said to me, "Will you accompany me?"
30. He said to me, "Leave the room and do not return."
31. The mother said to her boy, "Where have you been all the afternoon?"
32. Hari said to Rama, "Have you read the letter?"
33. The King said to the philosopher, "Whom do you consider the happiest man living?"
34. The magistrate said to the prisoner, "What are you doing with your hand in the gentleman's pocket?"
35. The fox cried out to the goat, "A thought has just come into my head."
36. He said to his sons, "Do not quarrel among yourselves when I am dead but remain united."
37. The lion said to the fox, "I am very weak. My teeth have fallen out. I have no appetite."
38. He replied, "I have promised to reward my soldiers. I have kept my word."

EXERCISE 109

1. Jack asked his mother to cheer up, because he would go and get work somewhere.
2. But the sea-god asked the prince not to be afraid and told him that he had taken pity on him and would help him.
3. The child replied that he would not kneel, for if he did, he would spoil his new breeches.
4. Alexander exclaimed that they were losing a good horse for want of skill and spirit to manage him.
5. Telemachus replied that he could not drive away the mother, who had born him and nourished him.
6. The philosopher replied that no man must be called happy until he had ended his life in a fitting manner.
7. The wolf asked the fox to yield himself as vanquished. If he did not, he (wolf) would certainly kill him.
8. He said that he believed that they were in that country among a people whom they liked and who liked them.
9. He asked them to take that bird away. Its guilded cage reminded him of his father who he had imprisoned.
10. The dealer told him that he had just one word to say to him. He must either make his purchase or walk out of his shop.
11. He thought that his hour had come and decided to meet death like a man.
12. Mentor asked him not to be cast down and to remember whose son he was. All would be well with him.
13. Bhishma asked the boys to remember they were playing a game. If it was Arjuna's turn he must have it.
14. The old man asked them to sit down and rest themselves there on the

bench. He said that his good wife Baucis had gone to see what they could have for supper.

15. The man exclaimed that he (the other man) did not know what those beans were. He added that if they were planted over-night, by morning they would grow right up to the sky.

16. He exclaimed that he was very clever. All his life he had been talking prose without knowing it.

17. She told her son that she was old and lonely and asked whether he had no pity on her loneliness. She asked him to stay with her, for he was yet more boy than man.

18. Goldsmith once said that he did not practise but made it a rule to prescribe only for his friends. Beauclerk, addressing him as dear doctor, asked him to alter the rule, and prescribe only for his enemies.

19. He asked who he was to speak to him like that and added that he was the master. He further asked why he should help him, for it was his work, not his (the speaker's), to draw the cart.

20. The duke said that he could not hope to see those trees which he was planting come in perfection, but it was right for him to plant for the benefit of his successors.

21. The king asked them whether they were angry because they had lost their leader. He said that he was their king and that he would be their leader.

22. An old Crab asked a young one why it walked so crooked and advised it to walk straight. The young Crab wanted its mother to show it the way.

23. The Deer asked the Jackal who he was. The Jackal replied that he was Kshudrabuddhi the Jackal. He lived in that forest all by himself; he had neither friend nor relation.

24. One summer some elephants were very much distressed by the heat and told their leader that they were absolutely perishing, for want of water. The smaller animals had bathing-places but they had none. They asked what they were to do and where they were to go.

25. When the king saw him coming, he asked who he was and what he wanted. The Rabbit replied that he was the ambassador from His Majesty Chandra—the Moon. The Elephant king asked him to declare his errand.

26. A young Rajah once asked his Vizier how it was that he was so often ill. He took great care of himself; he never went out in the rain; he wore warm clothes; he ate good food. Yet he was always catching cold, or getting fever.

27. He told his sons that a great treasure lay hidden in the estate he was about to leave them. The sons wanted to know where it was hid. The old man said that he was about to tell them, but they must dig for it.

28. Lady Grizzel remarked that Becky spoke French very well. Becky modestly said that she ought to know it as she had taught it in a school and her mother had been a French-woman.

29. The soldier asked the witch what she was going to do with the tinder-box. She replied that was no business of his. Since he had got his

money, she demanded that he should give her her tinder-box.

30. Ulysses said that his name was Noman and that his kindred and friends in his own country called him Noman. The Cyclops told him that this was the kindness he would show him : he would eat him last of all his friends.

31. Nelson told Hardy that he was a dead man. He was going fast and it would be all over with him soon. He asked Hardy to go nearer to him and said that his dear Lady Hamilton should have his hair and all other things belonging to him.

32. He called the shoemaker a big blockhead, as he had done the reverse of what he had desired him. He reminded the shopkeeper that he had told him to make one of the shoes larger than the other, and, instead of that, he had made one of them smaller than the other.

33. The Raja told the jester that he could extend no other mercy to him except permitting him to choose what kind of death he wished to die. He ordered him to decide immediately, for the sentence must be carried out. The jester said that he admired his kindness and chose to die of old age.

34. Her mother told her that she must go straight to her grandmother's cottage and not loiter on the way. There was a wolf in the wood through which she was going; but if she kept to the road he would not do her any harm. She asked her to be a good girl and do as I told her.

35. Next morning at breakfast his wife told George that she thought she could tell what was amiss with their clock. He sharply asked what it was. His partner replied that it wanted winding up.

36. A fawn one day told her mother that she was bigger than a dog, and swifter and better winded, and she had horns to defend herself. How was it that she was so afraid of the hounds? Her mother smiled and said that she knew all that fully well; but no sooner did he hear a dog bark than, somehow or other, her heels took her off as fast as they could carry her.

37. A young mole told her mother that she could see. So her mother put a lump of frank incense before her, and asked her what it was. The young one replied that it was a stone. The mother exclaimed that not only did she not see, but she could not even smell.

38. The princess asked the woman what she was doing. She replied that she was spinning. The princess exclaimed that it was very charming and wanted to try if she could spin also.

39. The judge asked the miser if the bag he had lost contained one hundred and ten pounds. The miser replied that it did. Then the judge concluded that as that one contained one hundred pounds it could not be his.

40. He answered slowly, asking his son sadly why he asked the one thing he could not grant him. His hands were too weak to rein those fiery beasts; he did not know the path. Therefore, he asked his son to ask something else, anything but that.

41. The speaker declared that he entirely objected to the proposal. He objected to it as founded on a wrong principle and as highly inconvenient at that time. He questioned me that they had considered all that the proposal involved. He entreated them to be cautious.

42. Kausalya forbade her child Rama to desire to possess the moon, because it was thousands of miles off, and it was not a plaything for children and no child had ever got it. If he wished she would bring some jewels that were brighter than the moon, and he could play with them.

43. The hen bird was just about to lay, and she asked her mate whether he could find her some place convenient for laying her eggs. He asked whether that was not a very good place for the purpose. She answered that it was not, for it was continually overflowed by the tide. Then he asked in emotion whether he had become so feeble that the eggs laid in his house were to be carried away by the sea. The hen bird laughed and said that there was some considerable difference between him and and the sea.

44. A cat, hearing that a hen was laid up sick in her nest, paid her a visit of condolence, and creeping up to her, asked how she was, what he could do for her and what she was in want of. He asked her to tell him whether there was anything in the world that he could bring her. He advised her to keep us her spirits and not to be alarmed. The hen thanked him and asked him to be good enough to leave her. She told him that she had no fear but she would soon be well.

45. He asked the child not to fret, for he could make her happier there than ever she could have been on the earth. He would give her beautiful things to play with, which a queen would envy. He promised that rubies and diamonds would be her toys, and her plates would be of solid gold. All the beautiful things she saw belonged to him, for he was the king of that rich underworld. But she only replied that she had been happy playing with the pebbles on the seashore, and she cared only only for the sparkle of the little waves on the shining sand. Saying that there were no flowers, no sun there, she wept anew.

═══ EXERCISE 110 ═══

1. is 2. has 3. were/are 4. was 5. has 6. was 7. is 8. have 9. has 10. is/was 11. was 12. was/is 13. was 14. is 15. eats 16. is 17. are 18. is 19. is 20. is

═══ EXERCISE 111 ═══

1. who 2. who 3. whom 4. who 5. whom 6. who 7. whom 8. who 9. who 10. who 11. who 12. whom 13. Whom 14. Whom 15. who 16. whom 17. who 18. whom 19. whom

═══ EXERCISE 112 ═══

1. Where is your luggage?
2. Can you give me some advice (or : a piece of advice)?
3. What beautiful scenery !
4. He has eaten two pieces/loaves of bread.
5. I have some important work to do (or : an important piece of work to do).
6. What awful weather!

EXERCISE 113

1. have (Subject is plural) 2. has (Subject is singular) 3. come (Subject is plural) 4. kill (Subject is plural) 5. were (subject is plural) 6. are (Subject is plural) 7. were (Subject is plural) 8. prevents (Subject is singular) 9. tend, themselves (Subject/Antecedent is plural)

EXERCISE 114

1. he 2. him 3. me 4. he 5. me 6. we 7. we 8. they 9. I 10. me

EXERCISE 115

1. As he was condemned to death the scaffold was erected for his execution.
2. Born in Surat, he received a part of his education in Mumbai.
3. Observing the house on fire, they sent for the engines.
4. As it was a wet day, I wore my mackintosh.
5. Having gone to bed very late, I was waken by the sun at about nine o'clock.
6. Referring to your esteemed inquiry, we state that the prices of the articles are as follows.
7. If one stands on the top of the hill, the eye roams over a beautiful landscape.
8. Having failed in the first attempt, he/she/I made no further attempts.
9. Bearing this in mind, we will find no particular difficulty.
10. Travelling from Karjat to Khandala, one finds the line most beautifully laid.
11. As I was his sole companion, he naturally addressed himself to me.
12. While we were crossing the channel, a heavy storm arose.
13. Hoping to hear from you, I remain yours sincerely.
14. When we called upon him yesterday, he subscribed a handsome sum to the Famine Relief Fund.
15. Going up the hill, we saw an old temple.
16. Resting in cool shelter, we beguiled the hours with desultory talk.
17. Information having been obtained, he was arrested for complicity in the plot. (or : having obtained information, the police arrested him for complicity in the plot.)
18. As we were weary with travelling, the destination seemed a hundred miles away.
19. When I met my friend in the park, he told me all the news.
20. When we/I entered the room, the light was quite dazzling.

EXERCISE 116

1. It was bitterly cold. (Adjective wrongly used in place of adverb)
2. I couldn't help laughing at the joke. (Double negative)
3. I remember never to have seen a more excited football match. ('never' misplaced)
4. This novel is very interesting. ('too' misused)

5. I am much annoyed to hear it. ('very' wrongly used with a past participle)
6. My friend said he remembered never having read a more enjoyable book. ('never' misplaced)
7. This hard won liberty was not to be lightly abandoned. ('hardly' confused with 'hard')
8. I am very glad to see you. ('much' should not be used with adjectives)
9. No one can write as neatly as he does. (Adjective wrongly used in place of adverb)
10. I cannot by any means (or : I can by no means) allow you to do so. (Double negative)
11. The flowers smell sweet. (quality of the subject, rather than of the action of the verb, is expressed)
12. I don't know anything (or : I know nothing) whatever of the matter,. (Double negative)

EXERCISE 117

1. For sale, a piano with carved legs, the property of a musician.
2. In a fit of peevish vexation, he tore up the tender letter which his mother had written him.
3. With thankful good humour the captain took the things which the gods provided.
4. Sometimes you will see an alligator eight feet long lying on the bank in sunshine.
5. All the day long, all the courtiers told the Queen how beautiful she was.
6. With her lap full of newspapers, Mrs. Jeremy Doud was sitting with her husband on the steps of the hotel, when Amy amd Dulce came up.
7. The man who utters such threats ought to be brought before a magistrate.
8. In his holidays he visited the battlefield where Napolean was defeated.
9. With a gun he killed the sparrow which was eating some crumbs.
10. No magnanimous victor would so cruelty treat those whom the fortunes of war had put in his power.
11. The constable said that the prisoner, full of rage and fury, seizing a bolster, had knocked the prosecutor down.
12. A nurse maid, about twenty years old, is wanted for a baby.
13. With a swollen leg I spent the last three days of my holiday in a chair.
14. This monument has been erected, as a mark of affection, to the memory of John Brown who was accidentally shot by his brother.
15. In thirty-seven wrecks, fortunately only five lives were lost.
16. The following verses were written, for his own amusement, by a young man who has long since been dead.
17. Owing to lack of fuel, many work must close if the strike lasts over the weekend.
18. In the long room 4 o'clock, there will be a meeting of all boys who play cricket and football.

EXERCISE 118

1. With but little modification these acts were pushed through Parliament in spite of opposition.
2. The beaux, as well as women, of that day painted their faces.
3. Riding across the field of battle, he saw countless number of the dead.
4. They work only when they have money.
5. With a frown on his face, he refused to relieve the beggar.
6. His body was found floating lifeless on the water, by a fisherman, at a short distance from where the boat was upset.
7. He was very fond of her, more than once he thought of marrying her.
8. It is proposed to construct a bath 99 feet long for males.
9. One day the bird did not perform to his satisfaction certain tricks which he had taught it.
10. I have lately received from the author's son permission to print the following tale.
11. In a motor-car they left the hotel where they had been staying.
12. The Board of Education has resolved to erect a building, three storeys high, large enough to accommodate 500 students.
13. With absolute contempt he spoke of the notion that the national debt might be repudiated.
14. One of the combatants was unhurt, and the other sustained in the arm a wound of no importance.
15. Girl of nice manners and appearance, wanted for telephone.
16. He repeated the whole poem with perfect accuracy after he had read it only once.
17. Very fortunately, he was shot without effect by a secretary under notice to quit, with whom he was finding fault.
18. A clever judge would see a great deal better than a stupid jury, whether a witness was deliberately lying.
19. I was impressed rather by the manner of the orator than by his matter.
20. He was driving away in a coach and six from the church where he has been married.
21. Stories, which are of an entirely fictious character, have often been related of these animals.

EXERCISE 119

1. The necessity of amusement made me a carpenter, a birdcager, a gardener.
2. Speak clearly, if you would be understood.
3. Even a fool, when he holdeth his peace, is counted wise.
4. When we had dined, to prevent the ladies leaving us, I generally ordered the table to be removed.
5. My orchard was often robbed by schoolboys, and my wife's custards plundered by the cats.
6. Whenever I approached a peasants's house towards nightfall, I played one of my most merry tunes.

7. By conscience and courage, by deeds of devotion and daring, he soon commended himself to his fellows and his officers.
8. Wealth may seek us, but wisdom must be sought.
9. Beware lest thou be led into temptation.
10. Brazil, which is nearly as large as the whole of Europe, is covered with a vegetation of incredible profusion.
11. We judge ourselves by what we feel capable of doing, while others judge us by what we have already done.
12. Some are born great, some achieve greatness, and some have greatness thrust upon them.
13. I, therefore, walked back by the horseway, which was five miles round.
14. Read not to contradict nor to believe, but to weigh and consider.
15. The leaves, as we shall see immediately, are the feeders of the plant.
16. A public speaker should be cool, collected and precise.
17. Sir, I would rather be right than be President.
18. In fact, there was nothing else to do.
19. At midnight, however, I was aroused by the tramp of horses' hoofs in the yard.
20. Spenser, the great English poet, lived in the time of Queen Elizabeth.
21. One of the favourite themes of boasting with the Squire is the noble trees on his estate, which, in truth, has some of the finest that I have seen in England.
22. When he was a boy, Franklin, who afterwards became a distinguished statesman and philosopher, learned his trade in the printing office of his brother, who published a paper in Boston.
23. We had in this village, some twenty years ago, an idiot boy, whom I well remember, who from a child showed strong propensity for bees.
24. Margaret, the eldest of the four, was sixteen and very pretty, being plump and fair, with large eyes, plenty of soft, brown hair, a sweet mouth and white hands, of which she was rather vain.
25. A letter from a young lady, written in the most passionate terms, wherein she laments the misfortune of a gentleman, her lover, who was lately wounded in a duel, has turned my thoughts to that subject and inclined me to examine into the causes which precipitate men into so fatal a folly.

EXERCISE 120

1. In the old Persian stories Turan, the land of darkness, is opposed to Iran, the land of light.
2. History, it has been said, is the essence of innumerable biographies.
3. Attention, application, accuracy, method, punctuality and dispatch are the principal qualities required for the efficient conduct of business of any sort.
4. When I was in Delhi, I visited the Red Fort, Qutab Minar, Raj Ghat, India Gate and Chandni Chowk.
5. He was now in vigour of his days, forty-three years of age, stately in person, noble in his demeanour, calm and dignified in his deportment.

6. Your wife would give you little thanks, if she were present to hear you make this offer.

7. A high-bred man never forgets himself, controls his temper, does nothing in excess, is courteous, dignified, and that even to persons whom he is wishing far away.

8. All that I am, all that I hope to be, I owe to my angel mother.

9. We all, or nearly all, fail to last our "lease" owing to accidents, violent and avoidable as well as unavoidable disease.

10. Nuclear bomb testing fills the air with radioactive dust and leaves many areas uninhabitable for centuries.

11. In a strict and legal sense, that is properly the domicile of a person where he has his true, fixed, permanent home and principal establishment and to which, whenever he is absent, he has the intention of returning.

EXERCISE 121

1. As Caesar loved me, I wept for him; as he was fortunate I rejoice at it; as he was valiant, I honour him; but as he was ambitious, I slew him.

2. The shepherd, finding his flock destroyed, exclaimed, "I have been rightly served! Why did I trust my sheep to a wolf?"

3. However strange, however grotesque, may be the appearance which Dante undertakes to describe, he never shrinks from describing it; he gives us the shape, the colour, the sound, the smell, the taste.

4. "Perhaps," cried he, "there may be such monsters as you describe!"

5. Sancho ran, as fast as his ass could go, to help his master, whom he found lying and not able to stir. Such a blow he and Rozinante had received. "Mercy on me!" cried Sancho. "Did I not give your worship fair warning? Did I not tell you they were windmills and that nobody could think otherwise unless he had also windmills in his head?"

6. Modern ideas of government date back to the 1600s, when, for the first time, people began to question a king's right to rule, once thought to be god-given.

7. When I look upon to the tombs of the great, every emotion of envy dies in me; when I read the epitaphs of the beautiful, every inordinate desire goes out; when I meet with the grief of parents upon a tombstone, my heart melts with compassion; when I see the tomb of the parents themselves, I consider the vanity of grieving for those whom we must quickly follow.

8. They had played together in infancy; they had worked together in manhood; they were now tottering about and gossiping away the evening of life; and in a short time they will probably be buried together in the neighbouring churchyard.

9. "Take away that bauble," said Cromwell, pointing to the mace which lay upon the table. And when the House was empty, he went out with the key in his pocket.

10. One day, walking together up a hill, I said to Friday, "Do you not wish yourself to be in your own country again!" "Yes", he said. "What would

you do there?" said I. "Would you turn wild and eat men's flesh again?" He looked full of concern and, shaking his head, said, "No!"

11. When a great office is vacant, either by death or disgrace, which often happens, five or six of these candidates petition the Emperor to entertain His Majesty and the court with a dance on the rope; and whosoever jumps the highest without falling, succeeds to the office.

12. That familiarity produces neglect has been long observed. The effect of all external objects, however great or splendid, ceases with their novelty. The courtier stands without emotion in the royal presence; the rustic tramples under his foot the beauties of the spring, with little attention to their colours or their fragrance; and the inhabitant of the coast darts his eye upon the immense diffusion of water without awe, wonder or terror.

13. If you look about you and consider the lives of others as well as your own, if you think how few are born with honour and how many die without name or children, how little beauty we see and how few friends we hear of, how many diseases and how much poverty there is in the world, you will fall down upon knees and, instead of repining at one affliction, will admire so many blessings which you have received from the hand of God.

14. We thank Thee for the place in which we dwell, for the love that unites us, for the peace accorded us this day, for the hope with which we expect the morrow, for the health, the work, the food and the bright skies that make our life delightful, for our friends in all parts of the earth.

15. Androcles, who had no arms of any kind, now gave himself up for lost. "What shall I do?" said he. "I have no spear or sword; no, not so much as a stick to defend myself with."

16. "My quaint Ariel," said Prospero to the little sprite, when he made him free, "I shall miss you. Yet you shall have your freedom." "Thank you, my dear master," said Ariel. "But give me leave to attend your ship home with prosperous gales, before you bid farewell to the assistance of your faithful spirit."

17. "O master!" exclaimed Ananda, weeping bitterly, "and is all the work undone, and all by my fault and folly?" "That which is built on fraud and imposture can by no means endure," returned Budha.

18. "Wretch!" said the king. "What harm did I do thee that thou shouldst seek to take my life with your own hand?" "You killed my father and my two brothers," was the reply.

EXERCISE 122

1. Nothing is so easy and inviting as the retort of abuse and sarcasm, but is a paltry and an unprofitable contest.

2. Think how mysterious and often unaccountable it is—that lottery of life, which gives to his man the purple and the fine linen and sends to the other rags for garments and dogs for comforters!

3. The human mind is never stationary; it advances or it retrogrades.
4. The laws of most countries today are split into two kinds : criminal law and civil law.
5. Islam is one of the world's largest religions with an estimated 1100-1300 million believers. It was founded in the 7th century by Prophet Mohammed.
6. There is a slavery that no legislation can abolish : the slavery of caste.
7. Truly, a popular error has as many lives as a cat: it comes walking in, long after you have imagined it effectually strangled.
8. So far from science being irreligious, as many think, it is the neglect of science that is irreligious: it is the refusal to study the surrounding creation that is irreligious.
9. None of Telleyrand's mots is more famous than this : 'Speech was given to man to conceal his thoughts.
10. There is only one cure for the evils which newly acquired freedom produces, and that cure is freedom.
11. If you read ten pages of a good book letter by letter, that is to say, with real accuracy, you are for evermore, in some measure, an educated person.

EXERCISE 123

newspaper—**Noun+Noun**
football—**Noun+Noun**
moonstruck—**Noun+Participle**
turncoat—**Verb+Noun**
brand-new—**Noun+Adjective**
jet-black—**Noun+Adjective**
onlooker—**Adverb+Noun**
sooth-sayer—**Noun+Noun**
stronghold—**Adjective+Noun**
ice-cold—**Noun+Adjective**
worldly-wise—**Adjective+Adjective**
tempest-tossed—**Noun+Participle**
race-horse—**Noun+Noun**
ear-ring—**Noun+Noun**
cooking-stove—**Gerund+Noun**
over-dose—**Adverb+Noun**
fire-proof—**Noun+Noun**
top-heavy—**Noun+Adjective**
heaven-born—**Noun+Participle**
skin-deep—**Noun+Adjective**
wide-spread—**Adjective+Participle**
snake-charmer—**Noun+Noun**
life-long—**Noun+Adjective**
upland—**Adverb+Noun**

EXERCISE 124

(a)   **super**=above...superstructure, superfluous, superscribe
       trans=across...transmit, tranship, transatlantic
       con=with, together...concentrate, collect, combine
       sub=under...subdue, submarine, subway
       auto=self...autobiography, autograph, autocrat
       mis=bad, badly...misconduct, misbehave, mismanage
       ante=before...anteroom, antechapel, antediluvian
       post=after...post-diluvian, post-mortem, postscript
       vice=in the place of...vice-president, vice-chancellor, vice-principal
       extra=outside, beyond...extraordinary, extra-troical, extra-territorial
       pre=before...prefix, pre-arrange, pre-Shakespearear
       arch= chief...archbishop, arch-enemy, arch-liar

(b)   **-en** : wooden, woollen, leaden, earthern, flaxen
       -ish : boyish, girlish, childish, brutish, foolish
       -less : faithless, pitiless, merciless, hopeless, senseless

(c)   a little river—rivulet
       the state of being a child—childhood
       to make fat—fatten
       which cannot be read—illegible
       unfit to be chosen—ineligible

(d)   incredible—in=not
       antidote—anti=against
       anarchy—an=without
       misconduct—mis=wrong
       monarch—mona=single, alone
       sympathy—sym=with
       manhood—hood=state, condition
       hillock—small
       archbishop—arch=chief
       amiss—a=without
       bicycle—bi=two
       dismantle—dis=apart
       freshen—en=make (causative)

(e)   circumstance—circumstantial
       habit—habitual
       stone—stony
       miser —miserly
       irony—ironical
       Labour—Laborious
       circuit—circuitous

(f)   friend—befriend
       bath—bathe
       fertile—fertilize

   grass—graze
   clean—clean, cleanse
   sweet—sweeten
   critic—criticise

(g)   sustain—sustenance
      attain—attainment
      confess—confession
      attach—attachment
      fortify—fortification
      oblige—obligation
      give—gift
      cruel—hatred
      govern—government
      sweet—sweetness

(h)   muscle—muscular
      hazard—hazardous
      worth—worthy
      quarrel—quarrelsome
      admire—admirable
      thirst—thirsty
      god—godly

(i)   fortune—misfortune
      legible—illegible
      visible—invisible
      agreeable—disagreeable
      ever—never
      fortunate—unfortunate
      practicable—impracticable
      honour—dishonour
      patience—impatience
      sense—nonsense
      truth—untruth
      resolute—irresolute
      legal—illegal
      capable—incapable
      organize—disorganise
      credible—incredible
      creditable—increditable

(j)   in- = not (Latin)
      bene- = well (Latin)
      post- = after (Latin)
      dys=badly (Greek)
      dis=apart (Latin)

(l)   hale=heal

```
              glass=glaze
              high=height
              sit—seat
              dig—ditch
              strong—strength
              deep—depth
     (m)      grand—grandeur
              discreet—discretion
              supreme—supremacy
              rival—rivalry
              certain—certainly
              warm—warmth
              desolate—desolation
              dense—density
```

EXERCISE 125

1. Epigram 2. Irony 3. Apostrophe 4. Personification 5. Epigram
6. Interrogation 7. Synecdoche 8. Climax 9. Exclamation 10. Epigram
11. Interrogation 12. Antithesis 13. Litotes 14. Metonymy 15. Irony
16. Oxymoron 17. Apostrophe 18. Interrogation 19. Simile 20. Hyperbole
21. Synecdoche 22. Paradox 23. Epigram 24. Personification; Transferred
Epithet 25. Metaphor 26. Epigram 27. Interrogation 28. Apostrophe
29. Antithesis 30. Irony 31. Climax 32. Simile 33. Synecdoche
34. Hyperbole 35. Metaphor 36. Epigram 37. Synecdoche 38. Apostrophe
39. Epigram 40. Apostrophe 41. Antithesis 42. Antithesis 43. Simile
44. Personification 45. Antithesis 46. Simile 47. Pun 48. Apostrophe
49. Personification 50. Simile 51. Simile 52. Epigram 53. Metonymy
54. Apostrophe 55. Hyperbole 56. Anticlimax 57. Oxymoron 58. Antithesis
59. Epigram 60. Epigram.

EXERCISE 126

Pattern 1

	Subject	Verb
1.	Fishes	swim
2.	Dogs	bark
3.	It	is raining
4.	The sun	is shining
5.	I	agree

Pattern 2

	Subject+Verb	Subject Complement
1.	My father is	a doctor.
2.	She looks	ill.
3.	Isn't it	beautiful?
4.	Is this pen	yours?
5.	It was	dark.

Pattern 3

	Subject+Verb	Direct Object
1.	I have lost	my purse.
2.	He knows	me.
3.	Close	the window.
4.	My uncle built	a house.
5.	I borrowed	his scooter.

Pattern 4

	Subject+Verb	Indirect Object	Direct Object
1.	He teaches	us	physics.
2.	His father promises	him	a present.
3.	Please pass	me	the salt.
4.	Shall I tell	you	a story?
5.	I wished	him	'Good morning'.

Pattern 5

	Subject+Verb	Direct Object	Preposition	Prepositional Object
1.	He bought	a watch	for	his wife.
2.	I owe	ten rupees	to	my tailor.
3.	Thank	you	for	your help.
4.	The fisherman saved	her	from	drowning.
5.	I must remind	him	about	it.

Pattern 6

	Subject+Verb	Noun/Pronoun	Adjective
1.	He painted	the car	blue.
2.	The boy made	his clothes	dirty.
3.	I found	the tin	empty
4.	She thumped	the cushion	flat.
5.	The noise drove	her	mad.

Pattern 7

	Subject+Verb	Preposition	Prepositional Object
1.	He believes	in	ghosts
2.	Look	at	that picture.
3.	I will arrange	for	transport.
4.	The police succeeded	in	catching the thief.
5.	The price depends	on	the quality.

Pattern 8

	Subject+Verb	to-infinitive (as object of the verb)
1.	I should like	to see the film.
2.	He wants	to talk to you.
3.	I forgot	to do my homework.
4.	We expected	to win the match.
5.	My uncle intends	to buy a car.

Pattern 9

Subject+Verb	Noun/Pronoun	to-infinitive, etc
1. She wanted	me	to help her.
2. They asked	him	to resign.
3. He didn't allow	us	to go out.
4. My friends encouraged	me	to compete in the race.
5. His father intended	him	to study for the Bar.

Pattern 10

Subject+Verb	Gerund, etc.
1. I enjoy	swimming.
2. He has stopped	speaking.
3. He likes	going to the pictures.
4. She avoids	meeting him.
5. They began	playing.

Pattern 11

Subject+Verb	Noun/Pronoun	Present Participle
1. We saw	him	opening the box.
2. I heard	somebody	laughing.
3. He found	Gopal	betting on horses
4. I felt	someone	moving behind me.
5. She noticed	the boy	going out.

Pattern 12

Subject+Verb	Noun/Pronoun	Plain Infinitive
1. We saw	him	open the box.
2. I heard	somebody	laugh
3. She watched	him	light fire.
4. The doctor made	me	take the medicine.
5. I felt	the mosquito	bite me.

Pattern 13

Subject+Verb	Noun/Pronoun	Past Participle
1. We found	your name	crossed out.
2. I got	my coat	pressed.
3. She had	her car	repaired.
4. He wanted	the speech	typed.
5. You must make	yourself	respected.

Pattern 14

Subject+Verb	Noun/Pronoun	(to be) complement
1. I thought	him	(to be) honest.
2. We supposed	him	(to be) a bachelor.
3. The teacher appointed	this boy	monitor
4. They chose	him	leader.
5. The jury found	her	guilty.

Pattern 15

	Subject+Verb	that-clause
1.	We thought	(that) he had left already.
2.	I expected	(that) you would get a first class.
3.	He suggested	(that) I should marry Kamala.
4.	She says	(that) she is very busy.
5.	The maid admitted	(that) she had stolen the watch.

Pattern 16

	Subject+Verb	Noun/Pronoun	that-clause
1.	Father told	me	that he would be back at six.
2.	He promised	us	that he would cooperate.
3.	I warned	her	that she shouldn't go alone
4.	Remind	him	that the meeting is on Tuesday.
5.	We informed	the manager	that we were willing to work overtime.

Pattern 17

	Subject+Verb	Interrogative+clause
1.	I asked	why he was late.
2.	We don't know	where he has gone.
3.	I wonder	whether he will attend the party.
4.	Please say	what you want.
5.	Can you suggest	whom I should meet?

Pattern 18

	Subject+Verb	Noun/Pronoun	Interrogative+clause
1.	I asked	him	where he had been.
2.	Please show	me	how I should do it.
3.	Please advise	us	what we should do
4.	Can you inform	me	where he is staying.
5.	They told	us	how well you played.

Pattern 19

	Subject+Verb	Interrogative+to-infinitive
1.	We must enquire	how to get there.
2.	I don't know.	what to look for.
3.	He forgot	where to turn off the main road.
4.	I don't see	how to stop him.
5.	She didn't know	which to buy.

Pattern 20

	Subject+Verb	Noun/Pronoun	Conjunctive+to-infinitive
1.	He showed	us	how to do it.
2.	Please advise	me	which one to buy.
3.	Tell	us	where to find a good hotel.

4. I have taught   him   how to swim.

5. Show   her   how to put it.

EXERCISE 127

1. isn't it ? 2. don't you ? 3. won't he ? 4. don't you ? 5. did I ? 6. are you? 7. haven't they ? 8. musn't we ? (Or : Needn't we ?) 9. will he ? 10. isn't he ? 11. is it? 12. has he? 13. won't they? 14. did he? 15. need I ?

EXERCISE 128

1.	(a) Yes, I can.	(b)	No, I can't.
2.	(a) Yes, I do.	(b)	No, I don't.
3.	(a) Yes, I am.	(b)	No, I'm not.
4.	(a) Yes, it is.	(b)	No, it isn't.
5.	(a) Yes, you are.	(b)	No, you aren't.
6.	(a) Yes, I does	(b)	No, he doesn't
7.	(a) Yes, I did	(b)	No, I didn't.
8.	(a) Yes, they will.	(b)	No, they won't
9.	(a) Yes, he is.	(b)	No, he isn't.
10.	(a) Yes, he has.	(b)	No, he hasn't.

EXERCISE 129

I.
1. Yes,/Of course they do.
2. Yes,/So/Of course he has.
3. Yes,/So/Of course she did.
4. Yes,/So/Of course they are.
5. Yes,/So/Of course he does.
6. Yes,/So/Of course he has.

II.
1. No, he doesn't .
2. No, I haven't.
3. No, he doesn't.
4. No, she didn't.
5. No, he can't.
6. No, he didn't.

III.
1. No/Oh no, he didn't.
2. No/Oh no, she hasn't.
3. But I haven't.
4. No/Oh no, he won't.
5. But he isn't.
6. No/Oh no, I am not.

IV.
1. (Oh) yes /(Oh) but I can.
2. (Oh) yes /(Oh) but she does.
3. (Oh) yes/(Oh) but he is.
4. (Oh) yes/(Oh) but she will.
5. (Oh) yes/(Oh) but you are.
6. (Oh) yes/(Oh) but you do.

EXERCISE 130

I.
1. So did Gopi.
2. So does his sister.
3. So must you.
4. So were bananas.
5. So has my brother.
6. So can his wife.

II.
1. Nor/Neither does my wife.
2. Nor/Neither could I.
3. Nor/Neither does that.
4. Nor/Neither was Wednesday.
5. Nor/Neither does her husband.
6. Nor/Neither did I.

III.
1. But I can't.
4. But she doesn't.
2. But my friend didn't .
5. But his brother doesn't.

    3. But I can't.   **6.** But English isn't.

IV. **1.** But my wife does.   **2.** But I do.

    3. But we will.   **4.** But others did.

    5. But she did.   **6.** But my friend did.

EXERCISE 131

(1)

	There+be	Subject, etc.
1.	There was	nobody in the house.
2.	There is	somebody to see you.
3.	There won't be	enough time.
4.	There is	a map on page 12.
5.	There isn't	much sugar in the tin.

(2)

	Subject+Verb	Adjective (expressing emotion or desire)	to-infinitive, etc.
1.	I am	delighted	to see you.
2.	He is	eager	to please the manager
3.	He is	afraid	to speak in public.
4.	We were	sorry	not to see you at the meeting.
5.	She is	content	to live in the village.

(3)

	It+be	Adjective	of+noun/ pronoun	to infinitive, etc.
1.	It was	unwise	of him	to accept the offer.
2.	It has been	kind	of you	to lend me you scooter.
3.	It was	careless	of her	to do so.
4.	It is	wicked	of him	to behave like that.
5.	It was	foolish	of me	to believe him.

(4)

	Subject+Verb	easy, difficult, etc.	to-infinitive
1.	English is	easy	to learn.
2.	This horse is	hard	to control.
3.	This poem is	difficult	to understand.
4.	Your question is	impossible	to answer.
5.	Our manager is	hard	to please.

(5)

	It+be	Adjective	to-infinitive, etc.
1.	It is	easy	to learn English.
2.	It will be	difficult	to reach the place.
3.	It is	bad	to bet on horses.

4.	It would be	hard	to please him.
5.	It is	pleasant	to work in this room.

(6)

	It+be...		Gerundial Phrase
1.	It's no use		applying for the post.
2.	It's no good		meeting him.
3.	It was no good		accepting the offer.
4.	It will be worthwhile		visiting the museum.
5.	It is foolish		behaving like that.

(7)

	It+be	Adjective/Noun	Noun Clause
1.	It is	probable	that he will arrive tonight.
2.	It is	surprising	that he should have failed in the examination.
3.	It is	doubtful	whether she will agree to it.
4.	It is	a pity	that they missed the train.
5.	It is	a mystery	how he escaped.

(8)

	It+take...	Time Phrase	to-infinitive, etc.
1.	It took us	two hours	to reach the place.
2.	It will take you	ten minutes	to walk to the post office.
3.	It took her	three months	to learn dancing.
4.	It has taken me	two years	to write the book.
5.	It may take him	a week	to finish the work.

(9)

	Subject+Verb	too+Adjective/ Adverb	to-infinitive etc.
1.	He is	too old	to walk.
2.	The tea is	too hot	to drink.
3.	They were	too tired	to walk any farther.
4.	I was	too busy	to attend the meeting.
5.	The thief ran	too fast	to be caught.

(10)

	Subject+Verb	Adjective/Adverb +enough	to-infinitive, etc.
1.	He is	rich enough	to buy a car
2.	You are	tall enough	to reach the picture.
3.	This novel is	short enough	to be read in two hours.
4.	The child is	old enough	to go to school.
5.	I drove	fast enough	to overtake him.

(11)

Subject+Verb	so+Adjective/ Adverb	that-clause
1. It was	so cold	that we cancelled the match.
2. He walked	so fast	that I couldn't overtake him.
3. The box is	so heavy	that he cannot carry it.
4. He was hit	so hard	that he fell to the ground.
5. She was	so clever	that they couldn't deceive her.

(12)

(i) What+(Adjective+) Noun	Subject+Verb
1. What a wonderful memory	you have!
2. What a silly idea!	
3. What a lovely song	(it is)!
4. What pretty eyes	she has!
5. What an ass!	he is

(ii) How+Adjective/Adverb	Subject+Verb
1. How lovely	the music is !
2. How pretty	the eyes are !
3. How beautifully	he writes !
4. How terrible	the noise is !
5. How wonderful	your memory is !

(13)

If—clause (Simple Present)	Main Clause (will/shall/can/may+plain infinitive)
1. If you telephone him	he will come.
2. If you eat it	you may be ill.
3. If you run	you can catch the bus.
4. If you come late	you will be punished.
5. If it is hot	we shall stay indoors.

(14)

If—clause (Simple Past)	Main Clause (would/should/could/might+plain infinitive)
1. If you telephoned him	he would come
2. If you took a taxi	you could overtake him.
3. If I were in your place	I would not agree to it.
4. If you didn't obey traffic rules	you might be put in jail
5. If I had the money	I would buy a car.

(15)

If-clause (Past Perfect)	Main Clause (would/should/could/might+perfect infinitive)
1. If you had telephoned him	he would have come.
2. If you had run	you could have caught him up.
3. If the driver had been careful	the accident would not have happened.

4. If he had taken the doctor's advice.   he would not have died.

5. If I had not been busy   I would have met him.

PARAGRAPH WRITING

EXERCISE 132

1. A Rainy Day

It was the first of May. Nobody had expected it to be a wet day. When I woke, it was so dark that I thought the night had not yet passed. In the meanwhile I heard the clock strike seven. I soon got up. No sooner did I come out than it began to rain hard. The rain poured continuously for four hours, so that the streets were flooded. For the past fortnight it had been intolerably hot, so the rain was a blessing to us. Who would not welcome a rainy day in the midst of scorching summer?

2. A Walk

Last Sunday, a friend of mine proposed that we should go to the seaside. I readily agreed. We could have easily gone on bicycles along the road. But we did not like to miss the romance and the beauty of the cross-country route. We proceeded on foot. In a few minutes we found ourselves in the company of nature. It was very pleasant indeed walking in the country. We were captivated by the sweetness and serenity of nature. We wished we had not reached the seaside so soon. Fortunately, while returning we lost our way in the woods, so that we walked nearly double the distance. There was a joyous mystery in roaming about in the woodland. Never had I felt such thrill of pleasure before.

3. The Cow

The cow is a very useful animal. She is very meek and gentle. She lives mainly on grass. In India she is looked on as a sacred creature and worshipped. She gives us milk, which forms an important part of our food. Her milk is the only food for children who are not breast-fed, and to them she is a second mother. She deserves our gratitude and kind treatment.

17. The Elephant

The elephant is the largest, as well as the strongest, of all animals. It lives on grass, leaves and roots. It is a strange-looking animal. Its peculiar feature is the trunk, which it puts to various uses. It draws up water by its trunk and squirts it all over its body. It can carry huge loads. It can pile timber. In Africa elephants are hunted mainly for their tusks, which yield ivory and are of great value.

21. Revenge

"Revenge, at first though sweet ,
Bitter ere long back on itself recoils"—

So says Milton. Revenge is an act of passion and often makes matters far worse. If you forgive your enemy's wrong or injury instead of avenging it, he will be ashamed of what he has done and you will have a spiritual victory over him. Forgiveness is the noblest revenge. We should not forget that we pray God to forgive us our sins.

STORY WRITING

EXERCISE 133

1. The Old Lady and the Doctor

There once lived an old lady, who lost her sight. She wanted to be cured of her blindness. She called in a doctor.

"I suppose I shall be able to cure your blindness," said the doctor, after examining her eyes. "I shall charge you Rs.1,000 for treatment."

The old lady thought a while. "I shall pay you the fee," she said, "only if my sight is completely restored. I shall pay you nothing in case you fail to cure me." The doctor agreed.

The doctor called at her house daily and carried on with his treatment. When he saw the lady's furniture he was tempted to steal it. Every day he took away some of her furniture. He delayed the cure till he stole most of her furniture.

At last the doctor cured her blindness. He asked for his fee. "I won't pay you the fee," said the lady; "the cure is not complete."

The doctor brought a suit against the lady. The judge studied the case. "Why have you refused to pay the doctor his fee?" the judge asked the lady. "Because my sight has not been completely restored," she replied. "I cannot see all my furniture."

The judge understood what had happened. He passed verdict in favour of the old lady. The doctor was not only to return the furniture which he had taken from her house but to forfeit his fee.

Moral : Dishonesty will be paid for.

2. Tit for Tat

A hungry jackal was wondering how to get to the other side of the river, where he could have plenty of crabs.

An idea struck him when he saw a camel. He went to the camel and said, "I'm sure you like sugarcane, don't you ?" "Yes, I do," replied the camel, "There is a lot of sugarcane on the other side of the river," said the jackal. "I'd very much like to come along with you. The river is so deep that I shall be drowned if I walk through the water. Would you mind carrying me on your back?" "Not at all," said the camel. "I am grateful to you for the information. I am very pleased to have the opportunity of returning your kindness."

With the jackal on his back, the camel waded through the water. On reaching the bank, the jackal pointed out the sugarcane to the camel and proceeded to eat crabs.

After finishing his meal, the jackal found the camel still eating sugarcane. He grew impatient. He was seized with an impulse to play a trick on the camel. He ran round the fields howling. The villagers heard the howl and rushed out. They saw the camel in the sugarcane field and beat him with sticks. The camel ran in panic and got into the river. The jackal at once jumped on his back .

While crossing the river back, the camel asked, "Why did you play such a trick on me?" The jackal replied, "I am used to howling after a good meal." "I am used to taking a bath after a good meal," the camel said and rolled in the river. The jackal was nearly drowned.

3. The Loyal Nurse

Once there lived a Rajah, who had no children for a long time. At last he was blessed with a son. Unfortunately, however, the Queen died in child-birth. A young woman, who had a baby of her own, was chosen as the prince's nurse.

The nurse began to bring up the prince and her own son together.

The enemies of the Rajah had been plotting to kill his son so that there might be no heir to the throne. They bribed the guards and entered the palace. A woman rushed to the nurse and warned her of the danger. The nurse had great affection towards her son, but her loyalty predominated. She quickly changed her children's clothes. Her own child was dressed as a prince. She left him there and escaped with the real prince. The rogues entered the room. The concluded that the nurse had run away with her own child. They murdered the child in princely robes and went away in exultation. The nurse thus succeeded in saving the prince.

The Rajah was greatly impressed with her sacrifice. He offered her great rewards as a token of his gratitude for her act. But she refused the rewards. Unable to bear her sorrow for her son's death she killed herself with a dagger. The Raja grieved over her death. He erected a magnificent tomb to commemorate her loyalty.

4. A Wise Judgement

Once a miser went out on business. He had a hundred pieces of gold in his pocket. When he had walked about two furlongs, he found that he had lost his purse. He was in great distress. He remembered that a few moments before he had taken his handkerchief from his pocket to wipe his face. He thought that his purse might have fallen on the road when he pulled out the handkerchief At once he walked back along the road but failed to find the purse.

The miser rushed to the town crier and sought his help. The town crier said, "You must offer a reward to the person who will return your purse. Otherwise you cannot get back the purse." The miser complied. He offered a reward of ten pieces of gold. The crier made the announcement.

A few days later a farmer came to the miser. "I picked up this purse while it was lying on the road," said the farmer. "Is this yours?" "Yes, it is," replied the miser, counting the money. "Thank you very much indeed for returning the purse," The farmer asked for the reward. "How dare you ask for reward?" said the mister. "There were a hundred and ten pieces of gold in the purse. You have already taken your reward." "No, I haven't", protested the farmer.

"The purse contained only a hundred pieces. You are bluffing just to avoid giving me the reward." The miser did not give in.

The farmer appealed to the judge. The judge heard the case attentively. The miser was summoned. The judge examined the purse. He turned to miser. "How many pieces of gold does your purse hold?" he asked, "One hundred and ten pieces," replied the miser. "But this purse holds only a hundred pieces," said the judge, "so it cannot be yours". He handed the purse to the farmer. The miser overreached himself.

11. Solomon and the Bees

King Solomon was known for his wisdom. The Queen of Sheba, who heard of his fame, once paid a visit to his court. She was very much impressed by his wealth and grandeur. She wished to test his power of solving puzzles.

She showed Solomon two garlands of flowers. She had one in the right hand and the other in the left. One garland was real and the other artificial. "Can you say which garland is real and which artificial?" she asked . The courtiers were puzzled. Both the garlands looked the same. Solomon could not say a word. The Queen felt triumphant. She thought Solomon would not be able to solve the puzzle.

Solomon soon ordered that the windows should be opened. A number of bees flew into the hall from the garden. They buzzed about the Queen and settled on the garland in the right hand. "The flowers in the right hand are real," said Solomon, "and the others artificial." The Queen was greatly impressed with his wisdom.

REPRODUCTION OF A STORY POEM

EXERCISE 134

1. Abou Ben Adhem

One night Abou Ben Adhem woke up to find an angel in his room. The angel was white and lovely as a lily and added to the beauty of the moon light in the room. Ben Adhem saw the angel writing something in a book of gold.

There was perfect peace, so Ben Adhem was bold enough to talk to the angel. "What are you writing?" he asked. "The names of those who love God," was the reply. "Is my name one?" said Abou. "No," replied the angel. "Then," said Ben Adhem more softly, but in a cheerful tone, "would you please put me down as one who loves his fellowmen?" The angel complied and vanished..

The next day the angel came again. It showed the names of those whom God blessed. Ben Adhem's name was the first on the list!

Moral : The best way of worshipping God is by loving one's fellowmen.

2. King Bruce and the Spider

I had been trying to do a great deed for the good of my people. I tried again and again, but did not succeed. I was disheartened by repeated failures. Sitting alone, I brooded over my misfortune for some time. I decided to give it up.

Just then a spider dropped from the ceiling. It was hanging by a silken thread . I wondered how it would be able to reach its web, which was a long way up. It began to crawl up the thread, but fell nearly to the ground. Again it tried to reach the ceiling and again it fell down. The spider did not seem ruffled. Again it crawled up and managed to go a little higher but fell again. It tried over and again with determination. It made nine vain attempts to reach its web. I thought it would no longer strive to climb. But to my surprise, it did try again. It was only a foot from its web. Slowly and steadily, it got higher and higher and at last jumped into the web.

"Bravo!" I cried out. "The spider did not give up in spite of repeated failures, and at last succeeded. I'd better try again."

I tried once again and succeeded.

5. The Blind Men and the Elephant

Once six men of Indostan, who were all blind, wished to find out what an elephant looks like. They approached an elephant one after another.

The first man happened to fall against the elephant's broad and sturdy side. "God bless me!" he cried. "The elephant is very like a wall!"

The second blind man felt the tusk. He found it round, smooth and sharp. "The elephant is very like a spear," he said.

The third man happened to hold the trunk. "The elephant is like a snake," he concluded.

The fourth stretched out his hand and felt the knee. "It's quite clear that this wonderful animal is like a tree!" he said.

It so happened that the fifth man touched the ear. "Even the blindest man can tell what the elephant resembles most," he said. "Who can deny the fact that the elephant is like a fan?"

The hands of the sixth man fell on the tail. 'The elephant is very like a rope!" he cried.

These six blind men quarrelled with one another for a long time, each firm in his own opinion. They did not know that they were all wrong.

8. Incident of the French Camp

The French soldiers stormed Ratisbon. The news had not yet reached Napolean. About a mile away, he stood impatiently on a little mound with his neck thrust out, his legs stretched out, and his arms locked behind.

He was perhaps reflecting what might happen to his soaring plans if his army-leader Lannes failed to capture Ratisbon. Just then a soldier was riding at full gallop towards him. On reaching the mound, he threw himself off the horse in joy and managed to stand erect by his horse. He had his chest shot through. "We have got you Ratisbon by the grace of God," he cried. "I have planted our flag myself in the market-place." The Emperor's eye shone, but soon moistened when he noticed the young soldier badly wounded. "You are wounded!" he exclaimed. "No," said the soldier, his pride hurt; "I'm killed!" He sank to the ground and died.

LETTER-WRITING

EXERCISE 135

1

20 B.N. Road
Thyagaraya Nagar
Chennai-600017
April 10, 2001

Dear Abdul,

My school is going to close from tomorrow for the summer. My brother who is staying in Hyderabad wants me to spend a few days with him. I am leaving in a couple of days.

Would you be good enough to lend me your camera for a week? I would like to have snapshots of Charminar, Mecca Masjid, Golkonda Fort and other historical spots and buildings during my stay in Hyderabad.

I assure you I will return the camera in good condition.

I hope you are getting on well. Give my love to Auntie.

Yours affectionately,
S. Ali Khan

7

32 J.N. Street
Allahabad
October 21, 2001

My dear Shyam,

I have just received your letter. I am unhappy to find that you have secured low marks in English, Hindi and Mathematics in your quarterly examinations.

I know you are intelligent. But what is the use of your intelligence unless you are industrious? How strange that you should get only 22 marks in Hindi, which is our mother tongue! It shows your gross neglect of studies. Realize what amount of trouble our parents are taking over our education.

I hope you won't waste your time any longer. Study hard and get good marks in the ensuing examinations.

With love,

Yours affectionately,
Ramesh Mohan

EXERCISE 136

2

852 Kachiguda,
Hyderabad-500027
March 1, 2001

Dear Gopal,

Thanks for your letter. You have asked me what my favourite hobby is. Well, my hobby is collecting stamps.

Since I was a schoolboy I have been collecting stamps. The stamps are in six fat books, so that I have a bigger collection than any of my friends here. The collection includes certain rare stamps, sent by friends in other countries in return for those which I sent to them.

Every two or three days I usually sit down in the evening at a table with my precious books setting new stamps in them and writing in the names of countries. The stamps can be not only delightful but also instructive. Each stamp has a story to tell me of far countries and strange peoples. Looking through the stamps, I can follow the history of nations with great interest.

Best wishes,

Yours sincerely,
V. Krishna Rao

EXERCISE 137

6

47 Shyamnagar
Hyderabad-500004
June 12, 2001

Dear Anand,

I got your letter yesterday. You have written me that you intend to spend a week in Hyderabad. I am very sorry indeed that I won't be here during your visit to this town. My parents and myself are going to make a tour through North India. We are starting tomorrow evening.

Though I am unable to keep your company, you are sure to enjoy your stay in Hyderabad. There are many sights worth seeing. You should not miss particularly Salarjung Museum, which is one of the biggest museums in Asia, Charminar, Mecca Masjid, Nehru Zoological Park, and Golkonda Fort.

All the best.

Yours sincerely,
P. Ashok Kumar

EXERCISE 138

1

20 Aswini Dutta Road
Kolkata-700029
April 24, 2001

My dear Peter,

I have reached Kolkata safe and sound. The train I boarded met with an accident, but luckily I was one of those who escaped injuries.

The train stopped at Kharagpur. When it was about to leave, a goods train which was coming in the opposite direction at full speed collided with it. Many of the passengers in the first two compartments died on the spot. It was a shocking sight. Some were severely injured. The casualities are estimated at 62.

I happened to sit in the last compartment. Nothing happened to me except that I experienced a violent jerk and fell on a passenger sitting in front of me. A few in my compartment had minor injuries.

It was found that the accident occurred owing to the signalman's mistake. He was immediately arrested.

Yours very sincerely,
K.R. Williams

EXERCISE 139

7

Visakhapatnam
December 8, 2001

My dear Kishore,

Your letter has arrived just today. I am pleased to hear that you are studying hard to get a first class in the examination.

But you should not be exclusively occupied with your studies. That can affect your health. You should also take part in athletic games. You may have heard of a sound mind in a sound body. It is no good reading all day. You will do well to set aside an hour or two every evening for games like football, volley -ball, badminton and tennis. Such games will make your body strong, prevent you from getting fat and keep you healthy.

I hope you will follow my advice.

Best Wishes,

Yours most sincerely,
N. Chandra Sekhar

EXERCISE 140

9

16 Dewan Road
Bangalore
February 12, 2002
Dear Ramakrishna,

May I remind you that you have not yet returned my copy of High School English Grammar and Composition borrowed from me a fortnight ago?

When you asked for the book, I said I am in the habit of referring to it nearly every day. I at last lent it after you assured me that you would return it in three days. You said you would send it through your brother, who was to come to this place on the following Sunday. You failed to return the book, probably because your brother didn't need to come here. Would you kindly make some other arrangement for the book to reach me?

With regards,
Sincerely yours,
K.V. Devender

10

24 Teppakulam Road
Tiruchirapalli
February 12, 2002

Dear Krishnan,

I am very sorry indeed to have failed to meet you yesterday evening. I didn't forget promising to call at your home at five yesterday, but I had to rush my brother to hospital as he slipped in the bathroom and hurt his leg. The doctor said it was a fracture. I was in the hospital till 9 p.m.

Joseph and yourself may have waited a long time for me. I apologize to both of you.

Yours ever,
K.V. Devender

EXERCISE 141

7

17 Giriappa Road
Chennai-600017
May 22, 2001

My dear Mohan,

In my last letter I told you that I was not satisfied with the house I was living in and was thinking of shifting to a new house.

I have at last managed to secure a better house. Last Sunday I shifted to this house. Not only is the house very spacious, but I have good neighbours here. Among my neighbours are two lecturers and a pleader. They are very kind to me and have proved to be excellent company.

I am sure I will be quite happy with my new neighbours.

Yours very sincerely,
G. Kishore Kumar

EXERCISE 142

1

82 Charni Road
Mumbai-400004
January 12, 2002

Messers Babcok and Singer,
Hill Road
Mumbai-400050

Dear Sirs,

I am sorry to have to make a complaint about the watch which I bought from you on January 7 (Bill no. 1432).

The watch does not show correct time. I have been using it since last Saturday, the day when I bought it. I have found that it gains four minutes a day.

I am sending you the watch through my brother. I shall be much obliged if you will either set it right or supply a new watch in its place.

Yours faithfully,
Rajendra Prasad

5

Dollops Bakery
Khairatabad
Hyderabad-500004
June 30, 2001

Dear Sirs,

I would like to let you know that I will be away on holiday for a fortnight i.e., from July 1st to 14th. Please do not deliver any bread during this period.

Yours faithfully,
M.A. Siddique

EXERCISE 143

1

15 Nehru Road
Allahabad
September 9, 2001

The Manager
New Press
Allahabad

Sir,

In reply to your advertisement in yesterday's **The Hindustan Times**, I wish to offer myself as a candidate for the post of clerk in your office.

I am 19 years old and have obtained a first class in the Intermediate examination. I have secured 62% marks in English. I am also good arithmetic. I am trained typist with a typing speed of 40 words per minute.

I enclose two testimonials, one from the Headmaster of the high school where I had studied two years ago, and another from the principal of the local Junior college from which I passed the Intermediate examination.

If I am selected I shall try my best to satisfy you by honest and devoted service.

Yours faithfully,

Dinesh Gupta

EXERCISE 144

1

62 Thambuchetty Street
Chennai-600001
May 18, 2001

The Director of Education
Tamil Nadu
Channai

Sir,

I would like to apply for the position of a teacher in the Educational Subordinate Service.

I am 23 years of age. I obtained a second class in the B.A. degree examination with Economics as the main subject. I also hold a degree of Bachelor of Education.

For the last two years I have been working in a local private school but would prefer to work in government schools.

I enclose herewith a testimonial from the Headmistress of the school where I am working.

I assure you that, if selected I shall serve with the utmost devotion and sincerity.

Yours faithfully,

P. Saroja,

EXERCISE 145

1

The Editor
'The Hindu'
Chennai

Sir,

Particularly for the last two or three months there has perhaps been no day on which road accidents have not occurred in Chennai . It need not be pointed out that the accidents are generally due to reckless driving. Lorry drivers in particular are guilty of rash driving.

The other day I was shocked to witness a dreadful accident in Burma Bazar. While an old woman was going in a rickshaw, a lorry, which was passing in the same direction at top speed, dashed against the rickshaw from behind with the result that the rickshawman and the old woman were crushed to death under the lorry.

I hope that the authorities concerned will take steps to prevent reckless driving.

Yours truly,

V. Mahadevan

EXERCISE 146

7

44 Ganesh Chandra Avenue
Kolkata-700013
July 5, 2001

Dear Sir,

I hope you remember that I have passed the Matriculation examination in the First Division. In spite of your advice, I have decided to discontinue my studies owing to financial difficulties.

I am going to apply for the post of clerk in the Public Works Department. I shall be grateful if you will kindly give a testimonial. I would particularly request you not to omit to refer to my participation in school debates, Social Service Camps and athletic activities.

Yours faithfully,

S.N. Ghosh

25.

(i)   WANTED : A second-hand typewriter. Must be in good working order, moderately priced. Please write, giving necessary details to Sri Krishna Type Institute, 27, Anna Salai, Chennai–600002.

(ii) FOR SALE : An Ambassador Car, 1990 model. Used for two years. Price Rs. 90,000. May be inspected at Messrs Rajan & Co., Pondi Bazar. For further particulars, please telephone 23242657.

(iii) MISSING : A white puppy missing for the last two days. A scar on its forehead. Reward of Rs. 50 to anyone who finds the dog and informs. Phone 8523092. Address : 74 Ranga Road, Chennai-600004.

S. Swaminathan

COMPREHENSION

EXERCISE 147

1

1.   The passage is written about Mahatma Gandhi.

2.   A Hindu is one who believes in Hinduism. An Indian is a native or citizen of India.

3.   He showed us the way to live and the way to die.

4.   He loved all religions and all nations. He believed in the essential unity of man. He devoted himself to the service of all men, more specially of the poor and the distressed everywhere. He always followed truth.

5.   Nehru suggests that Gandhiji was the beloved champion and leader of the people both of India and of Pakistan. This is corroborated by the spontaneous tributes that his death brought from the people of Pakistan.

6.   Truth meant a great deal to Gandhiji. His dominating passion was truth.

7.   memorials=those which serve to keep in remembrance; monuments
immutable=unchangeable
essential=important in the highest degree
estrangement=separation in feeling and sympathy
spontaneous=of one's free will
discrimination=ability to see or make small differences
dominating=having control or influence
Himalayan=very great

2

1.   People had to listen to "The Voice" of Mahatma Gandhi on account of its form and matter.

2.   People were made to become curious as to how they were governed and what they got from the taxes they paid. So they took an interest in politics.

3.   Politics was switched on to concern for the needs of the common people. The improvement of the lot of the poor, especially of the lives of the people of the neglected villages, was the goal of politics.

4.   The standard of living of the people of the villages was raised. Subsidiary occupations for the agricultural poor during the off season were found. The housing of the poor was improved. The age-old wrongs of the depressed class, like untouchability, were removed.

5.   (a) Things which ought to be done but omitted to be done and serious blunders committed in administration.

       (b) No longer in the exclusive hands of small aristocracy but passed on to the hands of common men.

3

1.   Bad temper is usually considered a very harmless weakness. It is spoken of as a mere infirmity of nature, a family failing, a matter of temperament.

2.   There are men and women who are all perfect, except for a bad-tempered disposition. Ill temper is often compatible with high moral character and is therefore referred to as "the vice of the virtuous".

3.   Sins of the disposition are worse than sins of the body. No bodily
      vice does more to un-Christianise society than evil temper.
4.   Bad temper can embitter life, break up communities, destroy the
      most sacred relationships, devastate homes, wither up men and
      women, and take the bloom off children.
5.   According to the author, there is no place in Heaven for bad-tem
      pered folk, because they could only make Heaven miserable for all the
      people in it.
6.   breaking up : destroying
      running : devastating
      scandalising : withering
      sowing : embittering
      easily or quickly offended : touchy

4

1.   The statistics are correct.
2.   There are cricketers who turn out mechanically; there is no colour
      in their play. It was so with Shrewsbury. He had technical perfection,
      but there was no enthusiasm, no sunshine in his play, no swift surprise.
      Thus in cricket many runs and much dullness are associated.
3.   To many players cricket is not an adventure; it is a business. They turn
      out runs in a mechanical way with the result that there is no colour, no
      enthusiasm in their play. This is why cricket is losing its lustre.
4.   Gaiety gives cricket its character.
5.   Cricket should be played in a spirit of adventure and unselfishness.
6.   Jam Sahib was a lively player. To him cricket was an adventure not a
      business. He never struggled to score or hoard up runs. His play showed
      his spirit of unselfishness and sacrifice. He never sounded dull and
      mechanical. It was a great treat to witness his play.
7.   (i)   Aim to be lively player.
             Look upon cricket as an adventure.
             Be unselfish.
             Try to effect swift surprise.
      (ii)   Don't struggle to hoard up runs.
             Don't be dull and mechanical.
             Don't look upon cricket as a business.
             Don't be selfish.

5

1.   It would be burdensome and inconvenient to pay in silver nickle, or
      copper coins, so the Government allows payment to be made in paper
      notes.
2.   Both are of equal value.
3.   We cannot have only paper money because (i) money must be some-
      thing so useful that everyone wants, (ii) the metals are the best form of

money, (ii) it would not be possible to print just the right amount of womey which would keep prices at their proper natural level. If too much money is printed, prices go up at once.

4. Money facilitates exchange of things.

5. When there is more paper money the value of money goes down and consequently the prices of commodities go up.

6. The Government prints only a certain amount of paper currency so as to keep prices at their proper natural level. If it arbitrarily prints too much paper currency, prices rise.

7

1. If an author has genius, he suffers the penalty of genius. If he has only talent, various cares and worries make life extremely miserable. He takes great pains to compose. He meets with continuous disappointment at his inability to reveal himself. Also he is often faced with the difficulty of gaining the public ear. A literary life is, therefore, mostly an unhappy one.

2. Young writers hope that they will become famous if they just throw that poem at the world's feet. They believe that they have only to get that novel printed to be acknowledged at once as a new light in literature.

3. No Editors and publishers are a practical body of men; they conduct their business on the hardest lines of a Profit and Loss account. They cannot therefore be sympathetic to young authors.

4. It would be generally difficult for a young author to have his book published. After his book is brought out, he should be prepared to face hostile critics.

5. An author should take no heed of criticism. He should not take criticism more seriously than the bye-play of clowns for a circus. He should not try to defend himself against his critics; he should be silent.

6. Sioux Indians : American Indians of a tribe now living in the Dakotas,
   Minnesota and Montanna
   abandon the profession of the pen : give up writing
   laurel-crown : honour won ('Laurel' is a shrub used by ancient Romans
   and Greeks as an emblem of victory and distinction) to run the gauntlet :
   to be exposed to severe criticism (literally to run
   between two rows of men who strike the victim as he passes) hounded
   to death : hunted to death, as with hounds

7. The pangs of composition : trouble of writing
   buoyed up by the hope : keep up the hope
   mere brokers : those who merely buy and sell for others
   thirsting for your scalp : longing to overthrow you (American Indians
   tear off the skin as a token of victory)

9

1. Unless we work we can have no money. It is therefore necessary to work.
2. No. There is not enough money in the country to make everybody rich if it were divided equally; each would perhaps get about Rs. 150 a year.
3. Just as, if Mont Blanc was flattened out and spread over the whole of France, the level of the land would be raised only by about six inches, so also it would make very little difference if all the wealth of rich men in the country (who are only a few) was shared out among the rest.
4. The job that suits you is the best job in the world. By doing your work, whatever it be, you are helping to produce the things which other people need and thereby doing you part in the work of the world. You must therefore embrace it lovingly.
5. Put your back into it : work at it with all your energy
   doing your bit : doing your tiny share of work.
6. The world is compared to a great machinery. Every man is like a wheel which, however tiny it may be, is essential for the running of the machinery, which is to provide for the wants of hundreds of millions of people.

10

1. Great thinkers must live and move on a high plane of thought.
2. No, a liberal education is not necessary to produce great literature.
3. The ideas, sentiments, and expressions in a great book are quite beyond those of ordinary working life with the result that the reader becomes conscious of the contrast and grows melancholy and disappointed.
4. A habitual meditation on the vast problems that underlie human life—thoughts of immortality, of the littleness of mere man, of the greatness of man's soul, of the splendours of the universe that are invisible to the ordinary traffickers in the street—these things make it hard to understand the average human being.

13

1. Yes, poets are dreamers. They dream of things that may come true.
2. Yes, a poet is a practical man : only he is ahead of his time unlike a logician or a scientist, who is abreast of his time.
3. Yes, dreamers are useful to the world, in that every forward step that man takes in any field of life is first taken along the dreamy paths of imagination.
4. Fulton dreamed the steamboat and paved the way for scientific wisdom to convert the vision into a reality of steel and wood.

5.   If the poet did not dream there would perhaps be no advancement in any field.

6.   The poet is concerned with the future and cannot at the same time pay his attention to the present. He is thus a specialist. He gives the scientist a flash of the future, which the scientist takes and makes over into a fibre of today.

16

1.   The artist enables us to see the beauty of the world.

2.   The artist lends his eyes to people so that they can see and appreciate the beauty of the world, which is God's artistic masterpiece. We often love things only when we see them painted.

3.   The majority of men do not see the beauty of things unless they have seen them painted. They see in Nature what art has taught them to see in Nature. So Nature imitates art.

4.   The artist's first duty is to love beauty. Unless he sees the beauty for himself first, he cannot communicate it to others.

5.   The surest key to the knowledge of God is to get hold of beauty, for beauty is the best interpreter of God to man.

6.   The artist's real function is merely to exhibit things. He should not prove things nor exhort men to good works.

7.   Art primarily consists in ideas.

8.   Art makes a sorrowful experience beautiful, and by making it beautiful, it makes it pleasant. Through this process sorrow becomes a joy.

PRECIS-WRITING

EXERCISE 148

1.   Patriotism

People of every country—Englishmen, Frenchmen, Germans, Italians and many Indians—think too highly of themselves and consider their country the best or the greatest. No country can be absolutely good, just as no man can be thoroughly good. We have to eliminate poverty and misery from our country. We have to keep what is good in us and discard what is bad. We should accept whatever good we may find in other countries.

6.   The Roc

Weary of a quiet life in Baghdad, I set sail a second time with trustworthy friends, contrary to my previous intention. One day we landed on an uninhabitated island. I had my meal and fell asleep. When I awoke the ship was not to be found. I was greatly distressed. I saw something white at a distance and walked towards it. I supposed it to be a white dome. It had no door and was very smooth. Its circumference was fifty full spaces. I found no means of entering it.

Suddenly the sky was darkened by a gigantic bird, which was flying towards me. I concluded that it was the roc and the great dome her egg. The bird alighted on the egg.

7.   Bad Habits

Bad habits, such as over-eating, drinking, or smoking, are very easy to acquire. One should fight against the force of habit. Even good things can be very harmful when done to excess. The wise man is conscious of his bad habits and checks them promptly.

The use of tobacco has spread almost all over the world. Those who have acquired this bad habit would hardly be able to get rid of it. Alcohol, which is commoner in cold countries than in hot ones, does nobody good in any way and should be avoided altogether particularly in India. Alcohol, even if taken in small quantities, tends to affect the health.

11.   Arabs in the Desert

Arabia is largely desert, with only sand and rock. In the desert there are a few scattered springs of water with green grass, fig trees and palm trees around them. Such shady places are called oases.

The Arabs who are not in the cities live in the desert throughout the year, shifting from one oasis to another. They eat figs and dates. Their horses are the finest in the world and are very dear to them. Camels are more useful to the Arabs; they carry huge loads for many miles across the desert.

13. Rip Van Winkle

In a village at the foot of the Catskill mountains there lived a simple and good-natured person named Rip Van Winkle. He was very popular with the women and the children of the village. He was particularly helpful to the children at their sports. He did not like working for profit. But he was always willing to attend to other's business. He used to run on errands for women. He led an easy life. His wife repeatedly pointed out his idleness and irresponsibility. He said nothing in reply. His only good friend at home was his idle dog, wolf.

22. The Advantages of Poverty

Poverty is wrongly considered an evil. The poor lead a happier life than the rich. The children of rich men are not so fortunate as those of poor men. The home of poverty, free from care and social envy, is characterized by love and unity among its members. Most of the great men on earth are those who have sprung from the ranks of the poor. To abolish poverty would be to destroy the soil upon which mankind produces the virtues conducive to higher civilisation.

EXPANSION

EXERCISE 149

1. It is a great loss to a man when he cannot laugh

Laughter is indicative of joy. A man who laughs radiates happiness and wins friends. One who is incapable of laughter misses the zest of life. Laughter can be the best tonic. A man who cannot laugh fails to attract friends, loses his health, grows pessimistic and deprives himself of any pleasure in life.

3. Slow and steady wins the race

This proverb is a reference to the fable of the hare and the tortoise. While the hare, confident of success, took things too easy, the slow tortoise plodded steadily on and managed to win the race. We should not be discouraged by the size of the task we have to do. If we do it little by little and steadily, we can achieve success. The following quotation from Ovid sums up the ideas : "What is harder than rock, or softer than water? Yet soft water hollows out hard rock. Only persevere."

4.　One who follows two hares catches neither

Do only one thing at a time. If you try to do two things at once, you will be able to do neither. If a hunter pursues two hares, he is sure to miss both. You must therefore concentrate on one thing or the other. If you have several bits of work to do, finish one and then proceed to the other. You cannot succeed if you attempt to do more than one job at the same time.

5.　A great city is, to be sure, the school for studying life

In a great city we encounter different types of men—the rich and the poor, the proud and the humble, the deceitful and the innocent, the rough and the gentle, and so on. We find there doctors, lawyers, teachers, philosophers, businessmen, loafers, and so forth; and men who come from different States and have different customs. If we live in such a city for a year or two, we shall be able to acquire a good knowledge of life. The various facets of life can be found reflected in a large city.

8.　Where there's a will there's a way

If you have the determination to do something, you are sure to find a way of doing it. There is usually nothing that is impossible to do. Napoleon, who rightly believed nothing to be impossible, ordered the army to march into Itlay. "Sire, the Alps," said the general. "There shall be no Alps," said the Emperor composedly. And no Alps came in his way. What may seem impossible will turn out to be easy to accomplish, if you go on to do it with determination. Goethe once said, "He who has a firm will moulds the world to himself."

11.　They are slaves who dare not be in the right with two or three

Every man has freedom of thought. A man's judgement may differ from that of others. Sometimes it so happens that only two or three are in the right while the others are in the wrong. If you are convinced that those two or three are in the right, you should not hesitate to join hands with them, whatever the consequences may be. Many of us have a tendency to suppot the majority, out of fear. It is slavish to be afraid of the majority and not to be with the few persons who are in the right.

12.　Great talkers are never great doers

Men who talk much are often those who do little. We come across many persons who are eloquent over great things and, when the time for action comes, make themselves away. Many of those who deliver wonderful speeches about patriotism do no valuable service to the country; and what is more, they try to defraud the State of its revenue by corrupt practices. Men of action do not talk much. Those who do nothing are usually the most talkative.

16. Tell me not, in mournful numbers, Life is but an empty dream

Do not say that life is an empty dream. It is wrong to think that life has no meaning or purpose. Life is real and purposeful. We are born, not to die, but to achieve something before we die. There have lived on earth eminent thinkers, statesmen, writers, and so on, who are admired all over the world. We should follow their example and strive to do something remarkable before we make our exit from the world.

26. Custom reconciles us to everything.

Sometimes we have to put up with something irksome or unpleasant. As time goes by, we shall be able to adapt ourselves to it so that it will become part of our life. Thus we can get used to anything. Suppose we shift into a house near a factory which keeps going all day. At first the noise of the machinery makes it impossible for us to sleep at night, but we find ourselves accustomed to it in the course of time.

32. Breathes there the man with soul so dead, Who never to himself hath said, This is my own, my native land?

It is difficult to find a man who is devoid of love for his motherland. Everybody is deeply attached to his motherland. When a man has stayed abroad for a long time, he naturally gets sick for his motherland and feels a thrill of pride and pleasure when he returns. If there should be anybody who is so spiritually dead as not to love his motherland, he is sure to fall into oblivion though he may be a man of high rank, of noble family and of abundant riches.

ESSAY-WRITING

EXERCISE 150

3. School Games

'All work and no play makes Jack a dull boy': there is a lot of truth in this proverb. Pupils should not always be reading. Unless they enjoy some form of recreation, they become stale and their reading suffers in consequence. Games provide the best form of recreation in schools. Pupils, after playing for an hour or two, can go back to their books mentally refreshed.

Games not only provide recreation for pupils, but make their bodies strong and keep them healthy. They give them valuable practice in making eyes, brain and muscles work together. The commonest of school games are cricket, tennis, badminton, football, hockey, volley-ball and kabaddi.

Games are also very useful for character training. In every game there are certain rules to be observed, and by observing the rules pupils can imbibe discipline. Each of the players learns to work for his team rather than for himself on the playground, so that he will later turn out an ideal citizen working for the good of country instead of only for his own benefit.

Games should therefore be made compulsory for schoolboys.

7. Popular Superstitions

Look how the world's poor people are amazed at apparitions, signs, and prodigies! — William Shakespeare

A superstition is an irrational fear of what is unknown or mysterious. It is founded on ignorance and illiteracy. People all over the world seem to have superstitions. Certain hours are believed to be auspicious and certain hours inauspicious. Charms and amulets are worn as protection against evil spirits. A comet in the sky is believed to herald the death of a great person. The hooting of an owl is supposed ominous, and so is the whining of a dog in the dead of night.

It is considered inauspicious to travel towards the north on Tuesdays and Wednesdays, and towards the south on Thursdays. Some persons do not pay or lend money on Tuesdays and Fridays; they fear that they will be reduced to poverty if they do. Sneezing is regarded as a bad omen; if anybody sneezes before a journey is to be begun or some important work is to be started, it is postponed. If a cat crosses the way when a person is proceeding on important business, he fears that he will not succeed.

In many European countries number thirteen is considered unlucky, so that many hotels do not contain rooms numbered 13. They believe that if 13 persons sit at a dining table, one of them will die in a few days.

It is unfortunate that superstitions still persist in spite of the advancement of science. All superstitions are obviously baseless and absurd and prevent us from making progress in life. Man is a rational being. He should not allow the clear stream of reason to lose its way into the dreary desert of superstition.

8. The Use and Abuse of Leisure

Leisure is perhaps as important as work . When we work continously, for several hours we feel very tired and, unless we have some break, we cannot carry on and our health may be injured. After a little relaxation, we can work more energetically and more efficiently.

We should take care to make the proper use of leisure. Those who are engaged in manual work should, in the leisure, do the kind of work which exercises and entertains the mind. Those who do mental or brain work—for example, students, teachers, writers—should spend their leisure time in physical and athletic activities. Pursuits different from our regular business provide adequate relaxation.

There are various hobbies for us to pursue in our leisure hours : stamp-collecting, drawing, photography, music, gardening, and so on. A hobby is a pursuit in which one is really interested and therefore proves to be an excellent recreation. Evening walks, particularly in congenial company, can also be a relaxation, in that they provide opportunities to refresh ourselves in the open air and enjoy the beauty of nature.

Unfortunately, however, many of us have a tendency to abuse leisure. They spend their leisure time in drinking, playing cards, betting on horses and so forth. We should avoid unhealthy amusement. To sit idle is another way of abusing leisure. Idle hands are liable to do mischief. An idle mind is the devil's workshop. We should therefore be occupied with something recreative in our leisure hours.

12. Travel as a Part of Education

Travel, in the younger sort, is a part of education; in the elder, a part of experience.
                                                                          —Francis Bacon

We can acquire a great deal of knowledge from books. But it is only second-hand knowledge. By travelling we come into direct contact with things that we wish to know. Our knowledge of distant land gained from numerous textbooks cannot stand comparison with that which a month's travel there would give us. Travel gives a character of experience to our knowledge.

By travelling we not only gain knowledge but broaden our nature. Like the frog in the well, the man who sticks to his home has a narrow vision of the world. As Shakespeare says, "Rather see the wonders of the world abroad than, living duly sluggarized at home, wear out thy youth with shapeless idleness." In the places we travel about we are able to encounter men of different temperaments, customs and habits and learn to deal with them. We also learn to adapt ourselves to new manners and customs. We cultivate caution, forbearance and tact. And that is one of the chief aims of education.

Travel also helps us brush up our knolwedge of a foreign language. If, for example, we travel about England for a few weeks, we shall be able to speak English better through our contact with native speakers.

20. My Favourite Hobbies

When we have worked continuously for some time we need relaxation. To pursue hobbies is the best way of relaxing. My favourite hobbies are gardening, stamp-collecting and photography.

I have loved gardening since my boyhood. I enjoy watering my garden every morning and evening. If gives me enough physical exercise and sends me back to my work with renewed zest and vigour. It is very amusing digging up fresh beds for new plants. I grow flowers as well as vegetables. I beam with satisfaction when I cast my eyes on my luxuriant garden. The sight of the lively garden is increasingly refreshing.

My second hobby is stamp-collecting. I have collected hundreds of stamps.

I have arranged them in five books. My uncle, who often goes abroad on business, has been helping me to collect rare stamps. He sends me foreign stamps from the places he visits. Whenever I have a little leisure, I sit down at a table with my precious stamp-books, arranging new stamps in them and writing in the names of countries. Each stamp has a story to tell me of distant lands and strange peoples. Looking through the stamps, I can follow the history of nations.

I also love photography. Whenever I go for a picnic or on an excursion or travel round a strange place, I take my camera with me and snap interesting objects. I have a number of valuable snapshots, some of them highly recreational.

EXERCISE 151

7.   An Important Day in my Life

It was March 25, 1998. That was the day when our school anniversary was celebrated.

The Governor was invited to be the Chief guest. Like many of my school-mates I was very busy making arrangements for the function. We decorated the school, particularly the auditorium, as well as we could. The auditorium, where the function was to be held, looked like a fairyland.

Just at the stroke of five the Governor's car entered the school campus. Accompanied by the Principal, the Vice Principal and the President of the Students' Union, the Chief Guest went to the dais and took his seat. In his valedictory speech the Governor stressed the importance of discipline among pupils.

The next item on the programme was distribution of prizes, which I had been eagerly awaiting. I was one of those who were to be awarded prizes on the occasion. I came in first in elocution competition. When my name was called I felt a thrill of joy. When I was receiving my prize, I heard the audience clapping. I shivered when the Governor shook my hand while giving me the prize. I thought it was a dream. When I felt the prize and looked at it, I realized that it was a reality. It was a book entitled *Lives of Great Men*.

That has been an important day in my life—a day which I can never forget. Whenever I see that book, it takes me back to the memorable day. I have read the book several times and every time I read it, it drives home H.W. Longfellow's well-known lines "Lives of great men all remind us we can make our lives sublime........"

35. Some Wonders of Modern Science

Science has been making great strides particularly for the last five or six decades. Man has worked miracles in the field of science and there seems to be nothing that he cannot achieve.

The most important recent inventions have been in the field of electronics and computers. Computers perform complex calculations in a fraction of the time that would have been needed in the past. They help to run businesses economically and safely. Aircraft and ships use computers to monitor things like geographical position and fuel consumption.

Electronic devices have made robots a reality. Many factories now have robots that do several tasks such as painting and welding. Engineers have also developed 'intelligent' robots, which can act as guards and firemen, and may travel into space to distant worlds.

For hundreds of years man had dreamed of travelling in space. That dream came true in 1961: a Russian, Yuri Gagarian, was the first man to travel in space. In 1969 Neil Armstrong became the first man to set foot on the moon. Hundreds of people have travelled in space, but unmanned space flight is much more miraculous. Unmanned craft are equipped with instruments to send television pictures and scientific information back to earth. They travel through the solar system and beyond, photographing planets. All the planets except Pluto (the most distant planet) have approached and photographed.

Not many years ago, information could be carried from one part of the world to another only by cables under or over the ground, or be broadcast from radio transmitters. Today satellites are used in the world-wide network of telecommunications. Communications satellites are placed in orbit above the earth so that they can bounce radio signals from one part of the world to another. It is satellites that enable us to see on television events that are happening on the other side of the world a fraction of a second after they take place.

Rapid developments in modern medicine have conquered many diseases and disorders. The latest developments include body scanners, which can produce a detailed picture of the interior of the human body. Radio-therapy is often used to cure cancer. Today surgery is so advanced that surgeons can repair or replace organs such as the kidneys and the heart. Man has conquered nearly everything except death.

36. Educational Possibilities of Broadcasting

Broadcasting is one of the most beneficial scientific achievements. Besides being a source of various types of entertainment and recreation, it has a very important role in educating people, more particularly the masses.

By listening in to news one can keep in touch with current events. There are certain programmes on the radio which summarize, in the form of simple and interesting dialogues, current affairs so that even the illiterate can know what is happening around.

Speeches, discussions and symposia on a wide variety of subjects are broadcast regularly. Such broadcasts are of great educational value. For example, an opthalmologist introduces us to the structure of the eye and suggests precautions to be taken against eye diseases; a dentist points out the care of the teeth; a scientist expounds the theory of relativity; an educationist criticizes the present educational system and suggests measures for its improvement; a police officer talks about the methods of investigating a crime; a group of men of letters discuss the various aspects of Shakespeare's work; a doctor, a sociologist, an economist and philosopher give their views of family planning; and so forth.

The All India Radio arranges for farmers to be acquainted with the recent effective methods of agriculture by means of frequent broadcasts on the subject at nearly all the stations. It also broadcasts English lessons for secondary schools; the Central Institute of English and foreign Languages, Hyderabad, the Regional Institute of English, Bangalore, etc. help organize such English teaching programmes. The BBC's 'English by Radio' programmes, broadcast every night, are of particular value to learners of English.

AUTOBIOGRAPHIES

EXERCISE 152

5.   The Autobiography of an Elephant

I was born in a jungle. Till I was seven I had led a wild and free life with my companions.

One day a tame elephant entered the jungle. He offered to lead me to a sugarcane plantation. I was stupid enough to believe him. I did not know that he was a decoy, i.e., an elephant trained to lead his wild brothers into captivity. While following him I suddenly fell into a big pit. I had not noticed the pit as they had carefully covered it so that poor elephants like me could be caught. Such traps or enclosures are called `Keddas'.

I was left in that pit for nine days. I had nothing to eat. I grew terribly weak and, if I had remained there in that condition for two or three days longer, I would have perhaps starved to death. On the tenth day I was taken out of the pit and brought into a town. I was gradually tamed. I was trained to act as I was ordered.

My master treats me with kindness. He never neglects to meet my needs. He provides me with plenty of leaves, grass, roots and bulbs to eat. I help him in many ways. I carry huge loads for him. I pile timber. Sometimes he lends me to huntsmen. Hunsmen sit on my back and drive to the spots where they can find tigers and fire at them. Once I was lent to a Maharaja. That day I was painted with bright colours and covered with silk and velvet clothes. I was used in a state procession. With the Maharaja on my back I walked with an air of proud majesty.

I enjoy myself very much when I am led into a tank for my bath. I draw up water by my trunk and skirt it all over my body like a shower bath.

Though I have to live a life of captivity, I am not at all unhappy. I have learnt many things by living with men. My master takes every care to make me feel comfortable. I don't think my wild brothers are happier than me.

EXERCISE 153

16. The Autobiography of a Cobra

I belong to the genus 'Naga', the sort of snakes supposed to be highly venomous and characterized by the ability to flatten the neck into a hoodlike form when disturbed.

Till a few months ago I had been an object of dread. I wouldn't harm anybody unless they harmed me. If I am angry or frightened, I hiss and thus given men warning of my presence. Many men would have trodden on me if it had not been for the fact that I give a loud hiss when anybody comes near. Once a person trod on my tail in spite of my hiss and I bit him. He was the only person whom I bit. When he cried in pain, several men rushed to the spot and searched for me. I hid in a hole and escaped being killed.

Now I am quite harmless. One day I as caught by a snake-charmer, who removed my fangs so that I would no longer be poisonous. I am now his captive. I dance with my hood stretched as the snake charmer plays the flute. He shows me to people so as to earn his livelihood. He usually imprisons me in a basket. He does not give me enough food. I feel very miserable. Many times I have bitten that fellow, but to no avail, I am unable to take revenge on him as I have lost my deadly weapons (i.e., fangs).

EXERCISE 154

4. The Autobiography of a Parrot

I very much wish I were free again. I lie imprisoned in a cage. Whenever I see my cousins flying in the sky, I feel like joining them. My master is very kind to me and supplies good food, but I am unable to feel happy all the same. Six months ago he bought me from a fowler, who had trapped me in his net.

My master has taught me to speak a few words and sing certain refrains. Whenever he is tired and wishes to relax, he comes to me to hear me speak and sing. He goes back refreshed . I have learnt to say 'Good morning', 'Good evening', 'Good night', 'How do you do?' 'Thank you', etc. Very often I say one for the other as I don't know the meaning of the expressions. One day when my master had gone to the office, I heard his wife say repeatedly to her neighbour, 'My husband is a stupid'. Honestly, I did not know what the words meant. I repeated the sentences several times after my master returned home. Then he scolded his wife and beat her black and blue.

I recollect the delightful days I had spent before I was captured by the fowler on that ill-fated day. I used to lead a life of activity and adventures. I enjoyed flying to a great height and roaming among clouds. Sometimes I used to compete with my companions in flying and five times I came in first. when can I have such thrills of pleasure again?

DIALOGUE-WRITING

EXERCISE 155

2. Between a temperance advocate and a young man on evils of intemperance.

Gopi   :   Good afternoon, Mr. Shastri.

Shastri   :   Good afternoon, Gopi. Are you going to the pictures?

Gopi   :   No, I'm going to the Social Club.

Shastri   :   My goodness! Are you also a member of the Social Club?

Gopi   :   Yes, I joined the club just a fortnight back. Why are you so sur-prised?

Shastri   :   I have never expected you to join the club. What do you do there?

Gopi   :   We play chess, billiards, or cards for relaxation.

Shastri   :   I am pleased you have told the truth. Isn't drinking an evil?

Gopi   :   I don't think so—if one doesn't drink in excess. On the contrary, I consider it a jolly social custom. It would be discourteous and unsocial not to comply when my friends invite me to join them in revelry. It makes me lively and happy after the day's strenuous work. It revives me when I am tired. Drinking is a manly habit. Besides, it acts like a tranquilizer when I am troubled by cares.

Shastri   :   Well, you mean to say you don't drink in excess. Alcohol, even in small amounts, affects the liver and weakens the mental powers. It is a slow poison. All persons begin drinking only in small quantities and also intend never to drink heavily. But gradually they become drunkards and develop a persistent craving for alcohol, which would nearly be impossible to overcome. If you don't give it up now, you are sure to become a compulsive drinker in a few weeks— a literal slave to drink. It will not only damage your health but bring about a moral degradation, so that you will be hated and despised by your friends, your colleagues as well as your family.

Gopi   :   There is truth in what you say. I already notice a change in my wife's attitude towards me.

Shastri   :   Now that you are convinced of the evils of drinking, I suggest you mend your ways before it is too late. Drinking is not the only recreation : in fact, it can hardly be called recreation. There are several other ways of relaxing, when you are tired. Set an example to others by signing the pledges.

Gopi   :   Thank you very much for your timely help. Here is my pledge. I will completely abstain from alcoholic drink. (Writes and sings).

EXERCISE 156

10.   **Between a spider and fly**

Fly   :   What a beautiful house you have, Spider! Who has built it for you?

Spider :   It's so nice of you to admire my house. I have built it myself.

Fly   :   You have built it yourself? Where have you got that fascinating thread from?

Spider :   I spin the thread out of my own body. I have built a number of houses like this. The material is inexhaustible. I can go on producing thread till The moment of my death.

Fly   :   How strange! Would you please explain how you build your web?

Spider :   Certainly. I shall be very pleased to let you know the technique in detail. Please come in and have a cup of tea.

Fly   :   No, no! I am not too stupid to be deceived by you. You plan to trap me in your stickly web and make a fine meal of me, don't you? I know you are a cut-throat. You spin webs to capture innocent insects and make short work of them. Good-bye?

EXERCISE 157

1.   **The fable of "The Lion and the Mouse"**

Lion   :   (Waking) Who is this damned little creature that's running up and down my body? Is it you, wretches mouse? How dare you disturb the sleeping King?

Mouse :   I beg Your Majesty's pardon. It's only by accident that I've moved on Your Majesty's body.

Lion   :   I won't excuse you. You are under sentence of death.

Mouse :   O King of Beasts ! Please show mercy on this poor little creature! I shall be very grateful if you will spare my life. Some day perhaps I can do something to help Your Majesty.

Lion   :   Ha ! Ha ! Ha ! What an amusing braggart you are ! How can you— a tiny little mouse—ever do to help me? Anyway, I spare you your life : it is beneath my dignity to kill you. Go away !
         (After a few days the mouse finds the lion caught in a trap, tied with heavy cord.)

Mouse :   Very sorry to see you in this condition. I will try to set you free. (He chews through the ropes and sets the lion free)

Lion   :   Thank you very much indeed for helping me. I was foolish to laugh at you when you said you might be of service to me some day. Help in time of need can come from any course.

═══ EXERCISE 158 ═══

7.   Between two friends on a topic of common interest

Venu   :   I am surprised that Ramesh has got only a second class while Mohan has got a first class.

Madhu :   So am I. The present system of examination is defective and needs reforming.

Venu   :   Yes, I suppose so. It fails to discriminate between a bright hard-working student and a dull student.

Madhu: What is more, a dull student sometimes gets more marks than a brilliant student. That is exactly what has happened in the present case. Ramesh is very intelligent and hard-working. Mohan is only a boy of average intelligence. By memorizing a few select answers he has passed with flying colours.

Venu   :   Yes, he has. A student who sincerely reads the textbooks gets fewer marks than one who completely relies on bazar guides.

Madhu :   I notice another defect in the examination system. What the student has studied, for a year or two is assessed in two or three hours. This system tempted the student to put off his studies until the last month. He doesn't have to work hard throughout the year.

Venu   :   You are right. It would be advisable to introduce periodic tests which are spread over the entire academic year.

Madhu :   That is a good idea. Periodic tests would compel the student to hard work throughout the year. I also feel that the essay type questions should give place to objective type of question.

Venu   :   I quite agree with you. Objective testing would compel the student to read the text-books through. It would also help measure the student's ability accurately.......Oh ! It's time I was going. good night!

Madhu :   Good night!

7.   The advantages and disadvantages of life in a great city

Abdul :   Good morning, Mr. Kareem. It's long time since we last met. When did you arrive?

Kareem: Good morning, Mr. Abdul . I only arrived last night. I have come here on business. I hope to return home tomorrow. I hate living in a great city like this.

Abdul :   Do you? Many people coming from the country enjoy themselves so immensely in the city that they don't feel like getting home again.

Kareem: But I find little enjoyment in the smoky air of a city and all its noise and racket.

Abdul :   Of course, in a city you cannot have the clean air and the quiet of the country. but that's a very small disadvantage compared with the facilities provided by a city. We have in this city theatres, cinemas, concerts, well-equipped hospitals, palatial buildings, and so on. We have here a wide variety of articles to choose from, if we wish to buy anything.

Kareem : That's why people living in a city tend to become extravagant. Those who go in for cheap entertainments can naturally enjoy city life.

Abdul : You are not completely right. A city provides not only public entertainments but various things that stimulate your mind—public libraries, museum, zoological gardens, art galleries, and so on. City life is a great boon to young boys and girls in particular; they have the benefit of excellent schooling. Besides, the city itself is a school for studying life. In a city one comes into contact with men of different types, manners and customs.

Kareem : Yes, city life has certain advantages, too. I ought not to be so allergic to it.

▰▰▰ EXERCISE 159 ▰▰▰

7. **The pros and cons of lotteries**

Tom : Just my luck ! I have bought as many as fifty Tamil Nadu raffle tickets, but haven't got a single prize.

Jack : How unwise of you to buy so many raffle tickets ! Why do you waste your money on lotteries?

Tom : I don't think I am wasting my money. If I get a prize, I shall become rich. If I don't, I console myself with the thought that my money is going to be used for the welfare of the destitute.

Jack : Your case is different; you have decent income. What about those who are tempted to buy raffle tickets in spite of their very meagre income—for example, servants, scavengers, rickshaw-pullers? Do you imagine how many poor men starve to enable themselves to buy raffle tickets?

Tom : As a matter of fact, I also feel the pinch of it, in spite of my decent income. I have been spending about thirty rupees on the average every month on lotteries. I have nevery won a prize.

Jack : It's true the money saved through lotteries is used for the welfare of the poor, but lottery is not better than gambling. It can have a demoralizing effect. It gives the impression that one need not work at all to become rich.

Tom : So it does. It has never occurred to me that lottery is an evil.

EXERCISE 160

2.   **Is poverty a handicap?**

Kishore :   Why does Mr. Joshi look so unhappy? He is a millionaire and has no cause to worry.

Ashok :   Do you think those who have plenty of money can be happy and get a lot out of life?

Kishore :   Yes. They can get whatever they want and make their life as comfortable as possible.

Ashok :   That's what most of us suppose. We don't realize that the rich are usually unhappy. We wrongly think poverty is a handicap. Many rich men wish they were poor so that they could be free from care and from social envies and jealousies. How sweet and happy the house of the poor is ! How loving and united its members are in the common interest of supporting the family ! There is more genuine satisfaction in life in the humble cottage of the poor man than in the luxurious mansions of the rich. Moreover, the rich are more prone to vices than the poor. Poverty is not a handicap, but a blessing.

Kishore :   Your words remind me of what Jesus said to his disciples : "It is easier for a camel to go through the eye of a needle than for a rich man to enter into the kingdom of God!" Many strong, eminent men have sprung from the ranks of the poor.

EXERCISE 161

Patient :   Good morning, doctor ! Can you spare me a few minutes?

Doctor :   Certainly ! Come in and sit down. Now, what is the matter with you?

Patient :   I've caught a cold, and I'm constantly coughing.

Doctor :   You aren't running a temperature, are you?

Patient :   I suppose I'm not.

Doctor :   Let me examine you...Your heart and lungs seem to be all right. Now open your mouth wide...Now breathe in deeply through the nose...There doesn't seem to be anything radically wrong with you. But you are a little run down. Take a complete rest. Get these tablets at a chemist's. Take two tablets thrice a day. You should be all right in three or four days.

Patient :   Thank you doctor.

Doctor :   Not at all.

THE APPRECIATION OF POETRY

EXERCISE 162

1. (a) The poet condemns the kind of life full of care, which allows us no time to enjoy the beauty of nature.

   (b) The 'stars' are the flowers that have dropped into the stream from the plants growing on the bank.

   (c) This is Personification. 'Beauty' is represented as a person.

   (d) A glance at a beautiful object gives us delight. If we continue to look at it, the delight redoubles. the personification employed above is continued in these lines. The poet speaks of the hectic life which allows us no time to stop for a while to experience intense delight when we see a beautiful object.

2. (a) The poet regards great books as friends who can always be relied upon. Their company delights him. They provide solace when he is in misery. He feels that he is greatly indebted to them.

   (b) They are the books which contain the minds of the great.

   (c) The poet's friends are the books. They can never part from him. They have been and will be helpful to him all his life.

   (d) The poet has often shed tears in gratitude for the books, which have been of great help to him.

3. (a) We should not think that whatever we have done or said is past and that we need not be concerned about it. Our actions and words have to be accounted for on the Day of Judgement.

   (b) The seeds which we scatter carelessly grow to be plants or trees and the seeds yielded by these plants or trees grow to be plants or trees in turn, and so on. So also the effect of our actions will remain for ever. The effects of our bad actions are compared to weeds and those of our good actions to beneficial plants.

   (c) We act and speak carelessly. We little know that our actions and words will last and have to be answered for on the Day of Judgement.

   (d) On the Day of Judgement we meet the dreadful consequences of our actions.

4. (a) The poet sees sweet content in high and low ranks. He finds it in some quiet place.

   (b) (i) Moths are spoken of as kissing their shadows on the lighted ceiling as they dance around.

   (ii) Heaven's bright face is represented as twitching with the innumerable stars.

   (c) (i) "Blink with the blind bats' wings": Here three words ("blink", "blind", "bat") begin with the same letter. This is Alliteration.

   (ii) "heaven's bright face........thousands there" : Heaven is personified. This is Personification.

   (d) 'Content'.

5. (a) Keats had read widely in English literature, particularly poetry.
   (b) Homer is profound and difficult to understand.
   (c) On reading Chapman's translation of *Iliad*, Keats felt like an astronomer when he discovers a new planet, or like Coretz when he stared at the Pacific with the eagle's eyes.
   (d) "Much have I travelled in the realms of gold"
   (e) "Pure serene" : spendid thoughts contained in Homer's work.
      "eagle eyes" : eyes as keen as an eagle's.
      "wild surmise" : thoughtfulness tinged with excitement.

PARAPHRASING

EXERCISE 163

1. Some people complain when they encounter a small misfortune in the course of their thoroughly happy life. On the other hand, there are some who feel quite satisfied and are grateful to God for His mercy if they come upon a small piece of good fortune during their miserable life.

2. If we study the lives of great men we are reminded that we too can achieve greatness and, when we die, leave behind us footmarks so that in future somebody who is desolate like a shipwrecked sailor may, on seeing our footmarks, have guidance and be infused with new life.

3. More things can be accomplished by prayer than people imagine. Let your voice of prayer, therefore, rise from the depth of your heart for me, like a fountain coming up from the bosom of the earth. If men, who have knowledge of God, do not lift their hands in prayer for themselves and for their friends, they are no better than sheep or goats, which are devoid of intellect.

4. This world is full of miseries. None can find here perfect happiness. Happiness, if it is found, is accompained with sorrow. It seems to be wise, and may not be an offence against the law of love, to compare our lot with the lot of those who are less fortunate, so that we may put up with our moderate misfortunes and sympathise with others who are more miserable.

5. We are all children of one and the same great God, whatever the place of our birth, our language, or our complexion. Even after death we shall not be divided according to our language, colour, nationality or country. Our common Father, from whom we our life and activity, is our impartial judge, to whom distinctions of race, colour or languages have no meaning whatever. He will judge us strictly according to our actions, good or bad, which he will assess with the utmost impartiality.

6. There once stood a school in that spot fenced with gorse that puts forth beautiful flowers, which there are none to enjoy. The schoolmaster, who taught in that noisy building, was a strict disciplinarian. He was fearful to

look at. All truants including the writer had experience of his sternness. Every morning, looking at their teacher's face, the trembling pupils used to forebode the misfortunes which the day had in store for them. He often cracked jokes and, whenever he did, they laughed with pretended joy. When he frowned, the terrible news was conveyed from one boy to another through whispers and circulated all around. Nevertheless, he was good-natured. If he was severe, it was because he was keen that his pupils should learn well.

7. It may be a weakness to love the place where we played in our childhood, but such weakness is praiseworthy. The man who is not moved by that scene is stone-hearted and incapable of being moved by anything. The wall on which we carved our names still visible; the bench on which we sat while fully occupied in reading, though it is damaged; the young children with their buttons unfastened, playing the same games on the same spot : all these are delightful to look at and call back to the mind our childhood pleasures. We seem almost to be sweet innocent children again.

8. Human activities are made up of trifles and half of our misery is due to our failings. The real joy in life is derived from peace and ease. Only a very small number of men can save or serve their fellowmen, but it is possible for all men to be amiable. Every rude person should realize that a small act of unkindness causes great pain. We may not find ourselves able to bestow plentiful gifts on others, but it is quite possible to restrain ourselves from offending them. We may not be able to give them large quantities of wealth, to favour them with high positions, or to give them perfect health. But we are endowed with the capability to console those who are in distress, pardon another for doing wrong, and resist taunts. God has ordained that happiness in life shall depend on these factors and misfortunes vanish when one has a true friend.

9. Now came quiet Evening. Twilight enveloped everything in grey light. There was silence. Beasts retired to their beds of grass and birds to their nests. The nightingale, which was awake, sang her love-song throughout the night. Her song was so engaging that silence did not mind being disturbed. The sky, covered with stars, looked as if it was adorned with sapphires. Hersperes, the leader of the stars, shone most brilliantly till at last the moon rose from behind a cloud in her queenly majesty and revealed her matchless splendour so that the world was enveloped in silver light.

10. If a person suffers misery as a result of his virtue, he deserves reverence. If his misery is due to some ill luck, he deserves sympathy. If it is due to vice he ought not to be affronted because his misery itself is perhaps a punishment proportional to his evil conduct. The nature of the man who censures a criminal about to be executed is not worthy of praise.

APPENDIX–II

Test 1

1. C	2. A	3. D	4. B	5. A	6. D
7. C	8. B	9. C	10. A	11. C	12. B
13. B	14. A	15. B	16. C	17. A	18. D
19. D	20. B				

Test 2

1. D	2. A	3. C	4. C	5. B	6. C
7. A	8. D	9. B	10. A	11. D	12. D
13. B	14. A	15. B	16. A	17. C	18. B
19. A	20. B				

Test 3

1. D	2. C	3. D	4. D	5. B	6. C
7. C	8. A	9. B	10. D	11. C	12. A
13. B	14. C	15. A	16. B	17. A	18. C
19. D	20. B				

Test 4

1. C	2. B	3. B	4. D	5. A	6. C
7. D	8. C	9. A	10. B	11. D	12. B
13. A	14. D	15. C	16. A	17. B	18. C
19. A	20. D				

Test 5

1. The vacancy has already been filled. 2. We keep the information on our computers. 3. I asked her what she wanted. 4. He wanted to know when I had arrived/I arrived. 5. He said, "I'll see you again tomorrow." 6. Everybody was present. 7. He was generous even to his enemies. 8. Although he was injured, he played in the match. 9. We were so tired that we couldn't walk further. 10. How about going for a swim? 11. What a clever girl (she is)! 12. He not only educated his nephew but also set him in business. 13. If you don't hurry, you will miss the train. 14. Sanjay doesn't work as/ so hard as Anil. 15. If we had some wood, we could light a fire. 16. If he had given me his number, I would have phoned him. 17. I wish I was/were a millionaire. 18. I wish I hadn't booked a seat on the train. 19. He admitted that he had stolen the watch. 20. I would rather you wrote on foolscap.

Test 6

I.   1. use 2. was invented 3. have been making 4. chew 5. is named
6. used 7. have never seen 8. turns 9. are ground 10. (are) mixed
11. presses 12. rolls 13. are cut 14. are planted 15. was made

II.   1. Can you give me some advice/a piece of advice, please ? 2. Let's
discuss the matter, shall we? 3. I usually go to bed at ten. 4. I had dinner
and watched TV for two hours. 5. I have known him for a long time.
6. My cousin lives in the USA. 7. Shall we travel by taxi or by train/ in
a taxi or on a bus? 8. I want you to wait here. 9. Both his sons have gone
abroad. 10. I haven't replied to his letter yet. 11. He told me/He said
that he wouldn't attend the meeting. 12. I suggested that he order/
should order more furniture. 13. Do I have to come next Thursday?
14. At last I was able/managed to make her understand what I wanted.
15. I have just phoned to congratulate him on winning the award.